THE BOOK OF
SMOKELESS FIRE

THE BOOK OF
SMOKELESS FIRE

S. Ben Qayin

Smokeless Fire

ISBN: 978-0-9905687-0-4

Published by Nephilim Press
A division of Nephilim Press LLC
www.nephilimpress.com

CONTENTS

BOOK I
ORIGIN OF DARKNESS

BOOK II
SUMMONING THE INFERNAL DJINN

Acknowledgments

irstly I would like to thank my holy spiritual father, Qayin Ben Samael, for instilling in me the strength and gnosis of the Eternal Black Flame that forever burns within. Special thanks goes to S., X. and L. for all their love and understanding through all. I also would like to thank all those who have stood by me and supported my work thus far, you all mean a great deal to me, and are never forgotten. As well, this project would not have been possible without the great help of the University of Toledo, Spain, which supplied me with invaluable information regarding the manuscript which this work is based on, Thank You. As well, I also greatly thank Robert Cook for truly bringing the art to life, his commitment to adapting the Djinn sigils etc. provided him was outstanding. I also wish to thank Nephilim Press, for their confidence in my visions, and amazing support. And last but not least, I would like to thank Robert Podgurski for his views on 'reality', and for supplying the insightful and generous preface to the current work, which has left me quite humbled. Thank you all…

PREFACE

"A little Learning is a dang'rous Thing;
Drink deep, or taste not the Pierian Spring"
ALEXANDER POPE,
'AN ESSAY ON CRITICISM'

ope's somewhat famous admonishment initially comes to mind as it touches upon the very real potential of this 'Book of Smokeless Fire'. On one level, S. Ben Qayin has undertaken a project of a fairly unique and perilous magnitude in extruding a grimoire of the 72 Infernal Djinn. And if that was all this text dealt with then it would fairly be cut and dry insofar as how to conceptualize it: primarily as a book of dark and infernal evocation. However, it is much more than that, subsequently begging careful consideration within the current milieu of modern magickal praxis. Besides his pioneering work into the evocational rites of the Djinn the reader can see that S. Ben Qayin has indeed helped to develop an intuitive approach to magickal architecture.

S. Ben Qayin's magical system outlined in his first book *"Volubilis Ex Chaosium"*, represents a refreshing and unique approach to the construction of the ritual circle and triangle of evocation that should prove insightful to almost any ritual magician. From my own perspective S. Ben Qayin's original methodology is bolstered by his attention to the interstices of the Akashic Light with regard to the magician's own body. And in an extremely telling fashion he brings attention to a meticulous and systematic formation of each angle of the evocational triangle, and the governing mind-body principles empowering it as such. He himself discusses the relevance of a grimoire insofar as when you read it and "know it will work" and "feel it is true." I will hazard to redirect this formulation and suggest that different sections of a book may themselves be selectively in synch with the reader. Furthermore, I would posit that even if the primary text is not entirely relevant to the practitioner that there are other certain important facets of this book that should not collectively suffer at the exclusion of the whole.

In drawing from the ancient *"Miscelaneo de Salomon"* S. Ben Qayin has developed a careful approach to calling forth these draconian spirits. There is an awareness on his part of the significance of regional aspects of these entities as geogamically specific forces. In conveying the nature of these spirits he refers to Castaneda's Yaqui philosophy of inorganic beings, ie, allies, in his delineation of the nature of these Djinn. We subsequently get the sense that these creatures of fire are not just spirits to be evoked and controlled via magical formula to serve one's beck and call but are entities that have *"shadowed"* our existence over time and have been accessible to some.

Magick born of necessity is the crux of S. Ben Qayin's endeavor here. This system demands a greater degree of responsibility in the hands of the magician than most other magical operations would have. To put one's self in the position of calling forth highly destructive forces necessitates a high level of introspection insofar as it is paramount to first acknowledge and identify these energies within. Otherwise, the tendency to be overwhelmed or obsessed is an all too present danger. The wrath within must first be harnessed before one can consider manifesting an exteriorization of such furies.

Ultimately, this grimoire is born out of a response to the greater question of unleashing destructive energies for establishing a sustainable magical order in the aftermath thereof. The rubble and scoria of creative destruction form the pieces of the puzzle that underpin reconstruction. This book is a direct challenge to the "Consensual Reality Matrix" and a practice for restructuring the network or web that is hung upon these nefarious foundation posts. As Peter Lamborn Wilson aptly describes in his TAZ:

> *"But now the lines are not all etched in time and space. Some of them exist only within the Web, even though they also interact with real times and places. Perhaps some of the lines are "non-ordinary" in the sense that no convention for quantifying them*

exists. These lines might better be studied in the light of chaos science..." (111)

For S. Ben Qayin the only approach to these lines is to grab them thus harnessing their pull through the engine of Chaos Magick itself, plain and simple. The incontrovertible need for this type of Magick is here whether we like it or not. And once one has read, considered, and meditated upon the premise and contents of this book, is it actually possible to close it and or shut oneself off to its inevitability? This is a vexed question that resonates through multiple registers; however, the primary issue in question is the matter of the truth and all of its precarious ramifications. As Pope concludes, *"Drink deep, or taste not the Pierien Spring."* This spring was said to impart inspiration to the muses, likewise *"The Book of Smokeless Fire"* represents a very dark wellspring for the aspiring Magician. Once stimulated, the thirst for this type of draught is as a strange awakened desire that should not be indulged except in the illuminating light of focused vision and a will forged of iron.

Robert Podgurski
7/15/2013

INTRODUCTION

he Necronomicon…A dream, a book, a nightmare. It is a tome which embraces absolute forbidden power that claims its ancient origins amongst the raging sands of the Arabian Desert. There, demons scream and lash about with great fury and terror. It is a book that tells of ways to conjure that which should not be, and gives means to command forces that exist outside of known universal laws. It bestows the ability upon the Magician to control fierce and destructive beings that are older than time, that are not of our Dimension, or Unified Field, but 'Outside' of it…

Many have sought this lost tome, for H.P. Lovecraft did not instill this idea in man, but awoke it from the dark recesses of his *'fragile eggshell mind'*. For in humanities veins lies the memory of its ancestors and archaic times, of fears and terrors that have been with the race since long before the dawn of the annals of its history. Lovecraft tapped his veins…and captured the lurid images that spilt out upon the literary floor as ink within the pages of his transcendent works. He wrote from inherit memory of strange times that have been shadowed upon our history, of twilight truths that the more common man rejects and turns away from in fear, replaced by a lighter more pleasant false reality that fits well within the confines of his limited existence of mediocracy and vision. Lovecraft felt the barriers of our universe, and that of others press uneasily against each other as bubbles being compressed. He knew of how delicate the barriers that separate the realities were, of the madness it all still is, and the insignificance of our small and simple lives in stark comparison to that which is magnificently ~ *'other'*.

Once this memory was brought forth to mankind from the depths of his dormant mind, it was never forgotten again. When men remembered, they became obsessed and began to search once more for the forbidden tome that none could clearly recall, only feel strong impressions of. Since Lovecraft wrote of the forbidden book, people began inquiring on where they may purchase it, as if it would be on a shelf for any passerby to put into their basket at the local bookstore. Of course Lovecraft proclaimed the truth, that the book did not exist, that it had come from a dream, though only because he had not found the tome, but the stark terror of its memory that resides in all of us as an echo of that which ought be forgotten, though is longed for. For who amongst man does not wish to embrace the forbidden ? To wield that which other men could not ? For the book promises wild power, and few have the want, or will, to resist it.

The work that is being presented within these pages is based on a very little known and overlooked Solomonic text simply known as *"Miscelaneo de Salomon"*, which amazingly mirrors that of Lovecraft's, *"Necronomicon"* both in content and history. It is an ancient and forbidden Arabian manuscript, that seems was later evolved into the Greek *"Goetia"* and gives the earliest known account of King Solomon and his binding of the seventy-two demons he sealed away in the infamous brass container.

The ancient diabolical manuscript was discovered in Spain, in the Mudejar Palace, *"Casa de la Encomienda"* of Ocaña Toledo province in 1969, while it was undergoing renovations to preserve and restore the palace. The cursed tome was discovered in a walled off secret room, buried in the floor so that it would be forever forgotten. Whoever placed it there obviously had a fear of destroying it, though sought to have no one ever recover it. The manuscript consists of 71 folios and dates back to circa 1428 C.E. It was hand written mostly in red ink with the remainder in sepia. This ink is still made today with the same ingredients in Morocco. The manuscript is written in older African Arabic that was common from around the 10th century and contains material on specific Angels ruling the hours of the day and night, the movement of the planets, instruction on the construction of talismans *(such as the "Picatrix")...and gives King Solomon's account of his binding of the infamous seventy-two sinister Djinn.*

The manuscript was first translated into Spanish by Joaquina Navarro and Juan Ruiz and published by the University of Granada Spain in 1987 by the title, *"Medicina, farmacopea y magia en el Misceláneo de Salomón"* or , *"Medicine, Pharmacopoeia and Miscellaneous of Solomon's Magic"*. It was again later translated into English by Nineveh Shadrach in 2007 under the title, *"Book of Deadly Names"*, which the present tome has utilized for the English translated names of the Djinn. As well, the descriptions given in this text are loosely based on the English translation, though much has been added through personal gnosis received from the Djinn themselves. The present tome is in no way associated with *"The Book of Deadly Names"*, as that text is an exact translation of the original manuscript. The present volume utilizes the true names of the 72 Djinn and offers a unique complex system for evocation of these entities, which has never before been released into the world. I have not provided the text itself within these pages, as it has already been translated word for word as mentioned, and feel it would be tedious. Though, I wished to instead take the forbidden information the original manuscript contained, and adapt it to be fit for the work of LHP Black Magicians. It has been brought to my attention that this text may appear to some as a 'copy' of *"The Book of Deadly Names"*. However this is simply not the case, any more than claiming Michael W. Ford copied the Goetia and called it his own, when he released any of his Goetic works. This is a work based on an ancient manuscript, that is all.

"Miscelaneo de Salomon" does not rest in a museum or library, but in the private collection of the owners of the palace it was discovered in; Rafael del Aguila Goicoechea and his wife Luisa Tejerina. Though the book contains nothing written of Lovecraft's Old Ones, it does deal with extremely destructive In-Organic entities that a Magician must bring forth, that have ancient diabolical origins. I don't believe a text will ever be unearthed that matches Lovecraft's description of the Necronomicon perfectly. That being said, the manuscript this work is based on, is as close as anything has ever come.

In Lovecraft's *"History of the Necronomicon"*, Lovecraft states the *"Necronomicon"* was said to have originated in Arabia, by the title, *"Kitab Al – Azif"*, or *"Book of Howling Demons"*, *Azif* meaning, the nocturnal sound made by insects supposed to be the howling of demons. It originated circa 700 C.E., and was composed by a Mad Arab named Abdul Alhazred. It was later secretly translated into Greek in 950 C.E. by Theodorus Philetas of Constantinople under the more commonly known title of *"The Necronomicon"*.

Being Greek in origin, the word *'Necronomicon'* has been examined thoroughly by numerous scholars, which have had varying ideas of translation, though it is generally agreed upon that the book's title pertains to the laws of the dead, or to those who would conjure and work with dark spirits, such as a Necromancer. One could view the work as the, 'Book Concerning the Dead' as cited by S.T. Joshi' in his foreword to Lovecraft's reprinted, *"The History of the Necronomicon"*.

It is easy to see the parallel histories between Lovecraft's Necronomicon, and that of the Greek *"Goetia"* now that this new manuscript has been brought forth from its darkness. Each volume originated in Arabia, were translated into Greek, are forbidden books that deal with dark and destructive entities that have their origins in ancient lore, and each were written by an Arab or Arabs, possibly mad with the knowledge they carried as a burden upon their backs concealed from all of humanity.

However, there is a vast difference between the resurrected manuscript and the Greek *"Goetia"* that came later. The text does not see the entities listed as demons, but as evil Djinn known as the *'Taw ~ All'*. Also, the names and descriptions of the Djinn are not the same as the demons listed in the later *"Goetia"*, but those that have never been known before, though there are similarities as far as the conjoined appearance of the entities is concerned; *'appears as a man with the head of a lion, having a monkey's tail'*, etc. As well, the ancient manuscript is not a grimoire, it only gives the account of the meeting between King Solomon and the Djinn and what transgressed, and it does not give instruction for use. However in that account, lie the very important names, descriptions and dwelling places, as well as the bane these Djinn cause. There are no methods for evocation, sigils or magical tools listed in this ancient account, which is why this present volume came into existence, to fill in the gap and bring these forbidden entities forth once more to turn the tides in this endless war against Order as much needed.

Of course *"Miscelaneo de Salomon"* bares a strong likeness to the earlier *"Testament Of Solomon"*, where King Solomon conjures forth the Demons of the manuscript through their representative, *'Beelzeboul; Prince of Demons'*, and asks their station, Angel of *frustration* etc., so he may bind them to construct his great temple in Jerusalem. And though *"The Testament of Solomon"* is considerably older in origin and far more known than *"Miscelaneo de Salomon"*, the latter of the two texts is marked as forbidden, and is derived and immersed in ancient Arabic traditions that happens to follow the history of Lovecraft's Necronomicon. For this reason, I have decided to concentrate solely on this little known material.

For historical value, it is also interesting to note the connection between King Solomon binding seventy-two Djinn into a brass vessel, and Arabian lore of Djinn appearing from a brass lamp to grant wishes. Indeed there were entities inside, but their ability to grant wishes was only half of the tale. *"Alf Laylah wa Laylah"* also known as, *"A Thousand Nights and One Night"* or *"The Arabian Nights Entertainment"* (a fifteenth century Arabic manuscript translated into English by Burton), is a tome that contains some of the earliest accounts of Djinn in written form. One story in particular titled, *"The Fisherman and the Djinn"* gives an interesting account of a fisherman catching a *brass container* in his net, *"..with the seal-ring of our Lord Sulayman son of David"* imprinted upon the top, and sets free an *'Ifrit'*, or Infernal Djinn which he must contend with.

> *"The fisherman accepted his (The Djinn's) promises on both conditions, not to trouble him as before, but on the contrary to do him service, and after making firm the plight and swearing him a solemn oath by Allah Most Highest, he opened the cucurbit."...*

> *"...There came forth from the jar a smoke which spired heavenwards into ether, and which trailed along Earth's surface till presently, having reached its full height, the thick vapour condensed and became an Ifrit, huge of bulk, whose crest touched the clouds while his feet were on the ground. His head was as a dome, his hands like pitchforks, his legs long as masts and his mouth big as a cave; his teeth were like large stones, his nostrils ewers, his eyes two lamps and his look was fierce and lowering."*
> ALF LAYLA WA LAYLA

Aleister Crowley speaks of the importance of *"Alf Laylah wa Laylah"* in his annotated version of the *"Goetia"* when he expresses how the magical work is equally as important to that of the Christian Bible and should be seen as such, though has not been exalted in the same manner, leaving it to himself to fulfill the undertaking,

"Even when we learn that the Bible, by a profound and minute study of the text, may be forced to yield up Qabalistic arcane of cosmic scope and importance, we are often slow to apply a similar restorative to the companion volume, (Arabian Nights) even if we are the lucky holders of Burton's veritable edition'...' To me, then, it remains to raise the "Alf Laylah wa Laylah" into its proper place once more."

ALEISTER CROWLEY IN HIS INTRODUCTION
TO HIS TRANSLATION OF "THE GOETIA"

This being said, it is clear Djinn have long been present in human history and have influenced much in religious beliefs as well as in magical praxis stemming from the Middle East. This newly recognized information that has come forth from, *"Miscelaneo de Salomon"*, gives rise to questions concerning the origins of the *"Goetia"*. Joseph Peterson covers this area well in his edited version of *"The Lesser Key of Solomon"*, though Colin Campbell explores the history a bit further back in his introduction to *"The Book of the Offices of Spirits"* which is clearly linked to the *"Goetia"*. However, though deeply researched, the true origin of the names and sigils in the *"Goetia"* are at this time, still unknown.

And though as illustrated, there are differences between *"Miscelaneo de Salomon"* and the *"Goetia"*, if one integrates this new information from the manuscript into the known history of the *"Goetia"*, we begin to see a progressive line of magical structure begin to establish itself. In the *"Miscelaneo de Salomon"* manuscript circa 1428 C.E., we see the very first Arabic account of the Infernal Djinn being presented to King Sulayman, whereupon they deliver unto him *(by force)* their title, habitation and the bane they cause mankind. Later, in *"The Book of the Offices of Spirits"* 1583 C.E., we see magical evocations added to this account so as to make the text useable to summon the demonic entities forth, though now the original Djinn of the Middle East were replaced by entities/Demons of a European origin. And lastly, we see the addition of demonic sigils, magical circles, triangles of arte and tools of all the separate elements of the first two manuscripts, finally compounded into part of a workable system known as 'Goetia' in the 1600's. Though, the text is much more suited for those who were/are akin to kneeling before the Judeo/Christian God, and not of one who seeks true gnosis of self deification. Regardless of the fact that in each of these tomes the infernal beings described and worked with in each, differ from one another by name and description, a clear connection between these texts can be seen and has been established.

When analyzing this history, one cannot overlook the Goetic system developed by Dr. Rudd in the 1800's that shows a direct connection between the Arabic Djinn and the European Demons. This system combines elements of both systems by offering the use of a drawn out 'brass container' *(featured in the Goetia)* that can be utilized in place of the more well known Triangle of Arte. Of course Rudd's Goetic Magic introduced the idea of summoning the 72 Demons by first summoning their opposing restraining Angels known as the Shemhamphorash. Whose names decorated the drawn out 'brass container'.

This information concerning Djinn came to me unexpectedly while researching for a now future release; I had no plans to write a book concerning Djinn. Some things simply cross your path and demand full attention. It seems it is time to release such a dark text. Seeing the importance of the work in connection to Lovecraft's *"Necronomicon"* and the Greek *"Goetia"*, as well as understanding that the names given were the oldest Arabic names of the entities that Solomon is so famous for binding, I felt the work must come forward to be known to a circle of Black Magicians that would see and appreciate the dark power that resides within.

As with my previous work, *"Volubilis Ex Chaosium"*, I have created an original operating magical system to be utilized here, that draws heavily from traditions based in the Middle East, while holding elements of traditional Western Ceremonial Magic woven in. As well, there are concepts presented here that are based in experimental theories that fall into a category I refer to as *'Fringe Magic'*. A Magic based on the manipulation of the Consensual Reality Matrix and the science behind it.

All of the Djinn sigils, Triangles and Circles of Arte, as well as Lunate Script, are of my own design, which were received when in a state of deep meditation, and are tuned to this specific current of energy. And as with *"Volubilis Ex Chaosium,* these systems I offer for utilization may be adjusted to the specific needs of the Magician to increase the potency of the rite by personalization. Magic must be personalized to be effective. So many magicians perform a rite with little to no success and wonder why. The reason for

THE BOOK OF SMOKELESS FIRE

their failure is that they were performing another's magic and not their own. A Magician must incorporate his own powerful elements into a working to build and harness energy that is sent forth into the Matrix of Consensual Reality so that it is altered in the Magicians favor.

I have thought long on this book, whether or not to bring it forth unto the world of men, for in it resides great pain and destruction waiting to be set free, much like Pandora's Box waiting to be opened. Though through much contemplation, I have come to the obvious decision to release this terror from its obscure and hidden origins for the sole purpose of spiritual balance. The world is in strife, though it is not Chaos that is the cause, but the ever oppressing forces of Order. Order is trying to control everything; right now we see this in our political system now that its dealings are becoming more and more transparent. Ironically, we also see this in the lack of news coverage concerning the forces of Chaos that fight back against this spreading control, because Order is suppressing it, the balance is not equal. Soon drones will fill the skies watching every movement; cameras are at every traffic stop. Order has the upper hand, and though Chaos is growing in power as we of the LHP grow in number and presence, I believe Chaos needs an influx of raw brutal strength and pure destruction to help overcome Order and establish a new spiritual understanding upon the Earth ~ *The Gates Of Hell Must Be Opened.*

I see this book as an equalizer…this text will help sweep the world clean in preparation of a new era unrestrained by religious dogma and corrupt control. It is to be unleashed against those who would uphold Order; it is to be wielded against those who would be happily dominated by it. It is to be brandished with no remorse and worked to destroy those who would stand in y/our way that are of the opposing RHP. It is to be used against those that are of the blood of clay born Abel. The book that lies within your hands is a weapon, it could easily prove to be one of the most diabolical works to date, and is the first of its kind in hundreds of years, if ever, to work with these particular entities in a manner that involves evocation and command. The beings that are conjured and worked with in these pages are of pure wrath, only offering the blackest deeds to be unleashed upon mankind without hesitation or mercy, at the sole command of the Black Magician.

All Necronomicons come with a warning, and though this book is not truly a Necronomicon, one will be given here none the less; This is a book

16

that lists the names and habitations, as well as the bane of seventy-two ancient and sinister blood thirsty Djinn of the Clan Of *'Taw ~ All'*. Unlike the "Goetia", these interdimensional entities cause only suffering and death to the human race. They are not here to help you find something lost, open locked doors, or turn you invisible…they are here to cause pain and to kill. They are extremely dangerous, and the utmost respect and caution must be implemented when dealing with them. There were cures/prayers listed in the original manuscript to counter the sinister deeds and inflictions these Djinn cause…I have not included them. One must be certain before summoning these Djinn, that the course of action they have chosen is correct, and stand by it.

It must also be said that I personally have not conjured all seventy – two for purposes of wrath, but for the creation of this work. Though the few I have summoned, feel completely different than Goetic Spirits. I strongly warn against calling up these Djinn without cause, they will surely get what they came for one way or the other, give them a target so it is not you who they seek. This being said, this work and system is experimental and dangerous, those who wield this gnosis do so at their own risk. It must be remembered that these dark entities have not been called upon in centuries. Those receiving this text when first released, will have the rare opportunity to call upon these horrendous entities, which have not been released for an ocean of time, before all others…great responsibility rests in your hands.

For the first time, in all its sinister glory, this forbidden gnosis is being presented to the Warrior Magicians who possess the blackest of hearts, who truly have the rage of vengeance that burns deep like a funeral pyre within the core of their dark soul. For whosoever wields this accursed book, is truly bound to the raging forces of Chaos eternal…

~ S. Ben Qayin

BOOK I

ORIGIN OF DARKNESS

THE HISTORY OF DJINN

ccounts of Djinn throughout Arabian history go back long before any written documentation, they seem to have always been, and spoken of amongst the Bedouin, who narrated tales and recited poetry that featured or mentioned them. Djinn were first written of in the Qur'an and within tales far older which made up the whole of *"Alf Layla wa Layla"*, or more commonly known as *"The Arabian Nights"* translated into English by Burton *(as mentioned before)*. The accounts of Djinn given in the Qur'an are numerous and provide some of the most detailed information regarding their origin and condition, as they dwell among men unseen.

According to the Qur'an Allah had created all, the planets and the stars, the Earth and the sea, the night and the day, and of course all the known and unknown animals and plants upon the Earth. He also created all spiritual creatures such as the Angels, Men and the Djinn,

> *"Allah created the heavens and the earth, and all that is between them, in six days"*
>
> QUR'AN (7:54)

All was well for an unmarked period of time. However, there arose a disagreement between Allah and some of his Angels, including his first and most beautiful Angel; Iblis. One day Allah decided to create Man to also walk upon the Earth alongside Djinn. When finished, Allah commanded the Angels to bow down before the newly formed Man and to prostrate to him. Allah said unto the Angels,

*"I am about to create man from clay: When I have finished him...
Fall ye down in obeisance unto him."*

QUR'AN (38:72)

Some Angels angrily questioned Allah and his action of creating Man and giving him violent dominance over the Earth, and even give indication of being horribly shocked at this act, questioning their own allegiance to him,

*"Would you put on Earth those who would spill blood ? And we
worship you ? And exalt you ?"*

QUR'AN (2:30)

It is here that Iblis had heard enough, for He knew that He would not bow down before man, nor would He again bow down before Allah, having seen the truth and awakening to His own Godhood, He knew He would never bow down before another again,

*"We created you and then shaped you. Then We said to the
Angels, "Prostrate to Adam," so they prostrated except for Iblis.
He was not one of those who prostrated. 'Allah asked, "What
kept you from prostrating when I commanded you ?" Iblis
stated, "I am better than him. You created Me from fire and You
created him from clay." Allah replied angrily, "Leave here, it is
not for you to become haughty here, now leave. You are among
the humbled." Iblis responded, "Respite me until the day that
they will be raised". Allah then said, "You are among those who
are respited." Iblis stated boldly, "Now, because you have sent me
astray, **I shall surely sit in ambush for them on Your 'straight
path', then I shall come on them and from behind them, from
their right hands and from their left hands. You will find most
of them thankful.**" Allah full of anger said, "Go now, despised
and banished. Those of them that follow you – I shall assuredly
fill Jahannam with all of them."*

QUR'AN (7:11-25)

It is interesting to note from Iblis's statement, That He does not intend to do mankind harm in general, only to those who are obedient to Allah/ Order and walk his, *'straight path'*. And so Iblis left his station of slavery, and raged upon the Earth in search of those who had chosen the *'Crooked Path'* of Darkness from among the Djinn, for Djinn had the ability to choose their individual spiritual path, and not all chose to be obedient to Allah.

There is a significant difference between the two classes of beings; Angels and Djinn. Angels are created solely to praise and serve Allah, while Djinn were to roam upon the Earth and have the freedom to travel their own spiritual paths through time, choosing either the way of slavery, *(As Allah himself referred to it)* or of independence, where one may walk the path of a God and know their own true strength and will.

As with human differences regarding religion, Djinn have many different clans and beliefs which they adhere to. One clan of Djinn were known to have listened to the Hadiths's *(teachings)* in the Qur'an being recited one day in a local town square, and found Allah's words to be true which led them to become followers of Islam. Though, as with human religions or beliefs, there were some Djinn which chose to be free of Allah's shackles, and follow the dark truth in their heart which lead them to reject Allah and his chains of servitude,

> *"Some of us are righteous, and some of us are otherwise: we are parties differing"*
> QUR'AN (72:11)

It was the Djinn that had *'deviated'* which Iblis sought, for they shared the same burning anger and hatred of Allah and his controlled society of slaves. And indeed Iblis did find them...and assembled an army of seventy-two of the most blood thirsty Djinn that had ever roamed the Earth.

Djinn were said to have been created before man *(of the element of Earth)*, from the burning element of fire,

> *"We created man from dried clay from black mud, and We created the Djinn before from the fire of hot wind."*
> QUR'AN (15:26-27)

Djinn have also been referred to being created from *"Smokeless Fire"* as The Messenger of Allah known as 'Muhammad' stated,

"The Angels were created from light and the Djinn were created from smokeless fire..."

There are some such as Ibn 'Abbas, Mujahid *(paternal cousin to Muhammad)* and others who believe that *'smokeless fire'* refers to only the very tips of the flames, or purest cleanest part of the flames, while according to others, it is *'flames mixed with the blackest of fire'*. Regardless, it is seen that Djinn are related to the Infernal spirit of fire and they are directly of its element. Fire and Djinn are synonymous with each other and entwined. Fire has long been associated with the spiritual world, acting as a gateway between realities and planes of dimensional existence.

An Ifrit is a class of very powerful Fiery Djinn which this volume directly deals with. Traditionally they are depicted as enormous fiery winged beings that are generally associated with walking the dark path of Iblis. They are mentioned in the Qur'an and *"Alf Layla Wa Layla"* among other lesser known texts *(at least to the Western world)* such as, *"Shams al-Ma'arif al-Kubra"*. However their description in *"Miscelaneo de Salomon"* is quite different, they are of the conjoined form most are familiar with as being presented in the *"Goetia"*. Some are simple in appearance, while others are complex and of horrendous conjuncture. The Djinn presented in this volume are Ifrit of *'The Clan Of Taw ~ All'*, known as containing the most purely destructive Djinn among the Houses, or Clans of Ifrit.

Of course when discussing Djinn, the subject of Ghouls must be included as they are indeed importantly related. It has been said that Ghouls *(Ghúl's)* are simply Djinn *(Jinn, Genie)* that did/do not follow Allah, and who feast on the blood and flesh of the living as well as the dead. Ismâ'il bin 'Umar Abū al-Fidâ', mentioned in *"Tafsīr Ibn Kathīr"* that Ghouls were the *'demons of genies'*, which further supports this.

There are many tales and descriptions of Ghouls or *'Si'lwah'* in Arabic history, and each has a different twist or take on the beings and their particular qualities, though there are some common beliefs that flow through them all, which leads to the credibility of the belief, as all embellished tales have a sacred truth that lies at their heart. One of these 'truths' tells of the use of a sword to slay a Djinn. Though other elements concerning the Djinn's circumstances and attributes differ from tale to tale, the belief that a single strike with a sword will kill a Djinn remains consistent. However if it is struck more than once, only a thousand more blows after that will cause it to perish, essentially making it invulnerable. In the tale *"Story of Prince Sayf Al-Muluk and the Princess Badi'a Al-Jamal"* from Burton's *"Alf Laylah Wa Layla"*, a Ghoul tries to trick a group of men that he captured and kept in a cave. One of the men freed himself and attacked the Ghoul by slicing it once across the waist with a sword. The Ghoul stated,

> *"O man, an thou desire to slay me, strike me a second stroke".* As the man was about to strike a second time, his companion advised, *"Smite him not a second time, for then he will not die, but will live and destroy us".*

This belief stems from a much earlier time when the Arab encyclopedic writer al-Jâhiz wrote that,

> *"The Si'lwah would die only by one mighty blow from the sword because if two strikes were directed to it, it would not expire until one thousand blows follow".*

Ghouls have long been associated with blood drinking and the dead. It is not uncommon to hear of rituals concerning bloodletting and blood as a source of energy when dealing in close work with dark spirits. In the French first translation of *"The Arabian Nights"* or *"Alf Layla Wa Layala"* by Antoine Galland, Galland is known to have added a bit of content throughout the corpus of the work, though mainly staying true to the original Arabic. However one area he added to, concerned the Ghoul and its nature. He stated,

> *"Ghouls were male monsters that in 'want of prey', will sometimes go in the night into burying grounds, and feed upon dead bodies that have been buried there"*
> 'THE STORY OF SIDI NOUMAN'

Though this is an added segment, *(which many believe to be simply a romantic horror element of the author)* I believe it was set there to give the reader a full understanding of the nature of the Ghoul based on older sources where Djinn reside in places of decay and shadow such as abandoned ruins, decrepit washrooms and of course, cemeteries. And from this, it is not hard to draw the connection between Djinn and Vampires and their numerous accounts and sightings throughout the dark history of man. Djinn have taken many forms and names in time.

Personally I believe that different regions of the Earth have various types of supernatural entities that are specific to those particular areas, just as it is with animals. Elephants are known in Africa, but not North America. A good example would be Banshees. Banshees are most commonly known to haunt or dwell in Ireland, and not in India. Or, there is the Zombie which is known to walk the land of Haiti as well as in some European areas such as Breton, but they are not known in Hawaii. In Hawaii there are Spirits which are only known there. Djinn are mostly known in Arabia and the Middle East, but since they are *(by their own description)* across the Earth, they are accessible to the Magician that is not close to the area of their main notoriety; Arabia.

It can be seen in the disclosures of the Djinn in *"Miscelaneo de Salomon"* that they dwell in all parts of the world, from mountain tops to oceans and everything in-between. And though these entities are not known by their Middle Eastern titles, they never the less have been recorded throughout history. It is interesting to note that though the Djinn/Ifrit/Ghoul, is most documented and centered in the Middle East, there are obscure references to them in the Western Hemisphere. One of the most important examples/ descriptions of Djinn from a Western source comes from Carlos Castaneda's series concerning the teachings of Don Juan, an Indian Toltec Sorcerer who mentors Castaneda in the arte of perception and awareness. They are described as 'Inorganic Beings' that dwell upon the Earth unseen, in cohabitation with men. Djinn are not specifically concentrated on in the series, however opening the eyes to 'see' 'Inorganic Entities' and hidden aspects of reality is. This is a segment of conversation between Don Juan and Carlos Castaneda on the subject,

"The counterpart of the Earth was what they (ancient Toltec Sorcerers) knew as the 'Dark Regions'. These (magical) practices were by far the most dangerous. They dealt with entities without organic life. Living creatures that are present on the Earth and populate it together with all organic beings"
Carlos Castaneda, *"The Fire From Within"*, 1984

Don Juan goes on to say,

"Organic living beings have a cocoon that encloses the (Eagle's) emanations. But there are other creatures whose receptacles don't look like a cocoon to a seer. Yet they have emanations of awareness in them and characteristics of life other than reproduction and metabolism."

These beings have made themselves known to man in different forms across the world, though only those who have achieved a heightened state of awareness and stored enough personal energy may perceive and interact with them,

"If those beings are alive, why don't they make themselves known to man ? I asked. (Don Juan replies;) 'They do, all the time, and not only to seers but also to the average man. The problem is that all the energy available is consumed by the 'first attention'. Man's inventory not only takes it all, but it also toughens the cocoon to the point of making it inflexible. Under those circumstances there is no possible interaction."

This 'heightened state' of awareness is brought on through many different mediums when used correctly, be it consumption of psychotropic/delic plants, intense pain/pleasure or hypnotic states of mind. The Sorcerer in this state is able to sidestep the perceptual filter that 'blinds' and 'see' the world in its totality so as to interact with entities that are 'In-Organic' by nature and achieve gnosis of a higher understanding of reality and existence.

Djinn are mysterious entities that have shadowed the human race since its beginning. The belief in Djinn is strong still today, though until now, the most diabolical have been inaccessible, hidden away from the eyes of those who would seek to again unleash their wrath upon the world. There are and have been, dark men who worship and work with Infernal Djinn who are aligned to the current of Iblis. For the Qur'an states,

> "We made the evil ones (Djinn) friends to those without faith (In Allah)."
>
> (7:27)

These men have practiced their rites in the shadows for centuries. It is in honor of these dark Sorcerers that this book is released and their dark tradition upheld.

Smokeless Fire

OUTLINE OF THE MAGICAL SYSTEM

any of the ceremonial aspects of the *"Goetia"* are derived and based on Peter de Abano's *"Heptameron"* which could indeed be considered a magical, Judeo/Christian manuscript. It becomes plainly obvious to any seeker that is of the LHP, that the system prescribed within the *"Goetia"* is not suited for LHP magic. Nearly all of the legendary *'Black Magic'* grimoires such as *"The Grimoirium Verum"*, *"The Grimoire of Pope Honorius"*, *"The Book of the Sacred Magic of Abramelin the Mage"*, *"The Grand Grmoire"*, *"La Dragon Rouge"*, *"The Sworn Book Of Honorius"*, *"Le Veritable Dragon Noir"*, etc., are unusable to any who were not devout subservient Christians, they were written from a Christian perspective. Yes, they indeed deal with the summoning of Demonic entities, but only in a manner that is abusive and degragating to the Spirits being called.

Michael W. Ford addresses this issue in his book, *"Goetia Of Shadows"* by reversing/adjusting the invocations/conjurations etc. in a manner suitable for Left Hand Path practitioners. Ford writes,

> *"The Lemegethon texts provided little for initiation as they are composed in a Christian structure. If you are other than Christian, this would be defeating to evoke a spirit of wisdom and power to then threaten it with the name of Yahweh!"*
> 'THE GOETIA OF SHADOWS'

Ford's approach is done in fashion of the traditional Black Mass, where the Priest/Magician reverses the Christian Mass by replacing Angelic names, names of God and religious imagery with those of Lucifer and his Demons, or by replacing traditional 'holy' items with those that were associated with the 'Devil', as H.T.F. Rhodes relates so well in his book *"The Satanic Mass"*,

> *"The priest goes to the church at eleven o'clock in the evening, and so times his Mass that it shall end on the stroke of midnight. His server is a woman with whom he should have been intimate. Prayers are said 'backwards'. A black three-cornered host and a chalice containing water are the elements of the offering. The water must be of polluted origin preferably taken from a well wherein an unbaptized child has been drowned."*
> 'THE SATANIC MASS, 1954'

Though Ford's approach is effective and based in solid tradition, this work will implement a new foundation to replace the Judeo/Christian influence, and focus on combining the spiritual *(energy work)* with the scientific *(Lovecraftian Quantum Physics)* to open gateways, so that interaction with non-human entities may be achieved. This is what I term *'Fringe Magic'*. Fringe Magic is simply *(and complexly)* mystical science. It is difficult to merge such areas of study, as science is so 'exact' and 'known', while mysticism or magic so, 'fluid' and instinctual, residing in the realm of 'un-known' or potential. Magic is subjective...by its very nature, it cannot be anything else. Magic is a balance of Chaos and Order; being completely Chaotic by individualization to be effective, yet having to adhere to the base laws of Order to be operational.

In order to work this particular kind of magic/science, one must be completely in touch with themselves and rely on their pure magical instinct. One must *'see'* or *'know'* what that magical instinct is. Ironically, that is the science of the magic. When you read through a grimoire and *'know'* it will work, when you *'feel'* it is true, as opposed to reading through one and *'knowing'* it is useless, and not worth the paper it is printed on – that is magical instinct. The Temple Of Set has classified using this kind of magical instinct to perform magical acts as, 'Medial Black Magic'. It is being in a state of 'Awareness', while utilizing the energies present at the random time the act is preformed. A.W. Dray describes this type of magic well,

> *"Medial Black Magic is a topic and discipline that is rarely if ever explored as a distinct art of its own. Most will touch and toy with its energies and potentials without knowing what it really is, but very few will grasp its true power and their own ability to wield it as part of their sorcery arsenal. Medial Black Magic is the spontaneous projecting of one's will and intent in conjunction with some form of physical action that is often spontaneous as well. It is of the highest forms of true Witchcraft and its methods and intricacies are always extremely personal. The sorcerer who suddenly utters the inspired words of an incantation into a passing wind to be taken away and made manifest or the Witch who gazes into the flame of a single candle and perfectly projects their will into the rising flame; these are examples of Medial Black Magic in motion."*
>
> 'THE INFERNAL PATH', 2012

Magic is ever present; it is the thread that holds 'All' together, it is existence itself. Opening the eyes to '*see*' and understand this has been crucial to any magical act true Magicians have ever preformed. One must understand that they are already in touch with the '*All*', all that is needed is to free the mind of doubt, and claim the power to alter one's personal surroundings by directing their Intent. Belief in the movement of one's personal energy, makes that energy stronger. All that is needed to change one's reality is to 'wake up', and direct their personal energy into that reality causing change, rather than just go along with the flow of the 'System'. Once this is realized, the Magician becomes master of his reality. Of course the more practiced and powerful Magician will cause more change in their reality than one who has just 'woken up' and began utilizing their potential. However, to cause change one must gather enough personal power to alter their reality, understanding is not enough to cause the change that is desired. The more one practices 'Magic', the stronger they become. As well, techniques of Vampirism have also been employed as a means to help gather such energy. Medial Black Magic is the Magician having full belief and confidence in themselves by transcending all natural laws and imposed laws/restrictions the 'system' has imposed, and directing their own Intent into their reality to cause the change that is personally desired. All of the Triangles of Arte and Magical Circles as well as the rites that are presented here, are a product of this same magical instinct. They were drawn from out of the 'Nagual' (*The Meon, Universe B, The Second Attention, Naxyr*) into existence on this plane for the use of the Black Magician.

Because these Djinn are '*Ghouls*' and they feast on the energy of blood and flesh, blood will be implemented in this system to draw them forth into the ritual chamber so they may feed upon it and empower themselves. The blood can be of any source, though it is thought proper to be the Magician's own blood that is used, as it connects the magician with the Djinn on an intimate level, thus ensuring more opportunity for success within the workings. Personally, I use blood in many rituals and workings, I always have. It is something very sacred to me. In my eyes, it serves as a sign of devotion as well as sacrifice. Within my spiritual beliefs, I kneel before no God, though offer them my essence out of respect and to empower the rite. I see all entities as being equal, some have been here longer than me and have more knowledge and experience, but that does not make them superior to me, only more learned. And, as such, they should know this and have the same respect for me, as I do them, equally. I offer them sacrifice, not out of fear, but honor and respect. I beg no entity or God to change things in my life, I ask them to help me as a brother, who walks the same Crooked Path as they do, and if I can help them in turn, then I gladly do. I have found that spiritual activity is greatly increased when blood is used in ritual. I find this because the energy that is being released by the Magician acts as a beacon in the spiritual world, attracting many different curious entities. It is such a personal offering that the Magician can fully immerse himself in ritual and the spiritual world, so contact with an entity is stronger and a bond formed. Naturally, blood is also used in a lot of sigil work I undertake. I believe blood helps to bring 'Life' to a sigil if created with it. This of course again connects the Magician with the spiritual entity that is being called forth, creating a pact of sorts as it is the essence of the Magician (*Blood*), conjoined with the essence of the Spirit (*Sigil*). Therefore, blood will be a central element when working with these particular Djinn in the ritual chamber, as well as when creating sigils, talismans, etc.

Suffumigation is also heavily drawn upon, it is and has always been a vital element within the magical praxis of the Middle East and so has been implemented within this system. Several different incense are used which include frankincense, myrrh and coriander seed. Frankincense *(olibanum)*, has been in use in Arabia for thousands of years, being a central element in both spiritual and religious praxis throughout its territory and history. There are ancient tales of the fabulous 'Atlantis of the Sands' *(as according to 'Lawrence of Arabia')* known as Ubar, Ad, Irem, Wabar…indeed Lovecraft's 'Nameless City', being a central point of trade for frankincense, within the vast sands of the 'Rub' al Khali' or Empty Quarter of Arabia. This remote and much needed location caused the inhabitants of this desolate city to become rich beyond imagination. That is, at least until it was devoured by the ground it stood upon by the command of 'God', due to the 'gluttonous ways' of the residents. Or so the story goes. Irem *(or what is thought to be Irem)* was actually found in southern Oman in 1992 proving the ancient tales, *(and Lovecraft)* true. Frankincense has also interestingly been found to be important in the Philistines' worship of the fish-god 'Dagon'.

Myrrh has also been used throughout Arabia. It is seen as a connecting agent to the Underworld and Death, or Chthonic Spirits in general, making it a fitting incense to incorporate within this system. And lastly there is Coriander Seed *(coriandrum sativum)* which has been used in many ancient Middle Eastern rituals centered around divination. Coriander seed has generally been associated with the planet Mars, and has its origins in the ancient Orient, it has been applied for many medicinal and magical uses throughout the ages.

> *"These (suffumigations and incense) are not just used to 'set the scene' but are an important and essential ingredient in the process of invocation and evocation, as 'spiritual creatures,' be they angels, daemons, spirits, demons, and even gods, respond directly to the correct use of incense"…"…the concept that burning enables you to pass something from this world to the other is never questioned. Hence the burning of incense, of the right kind, is also able to affect the denizens of the other world."*
> STEPHEN SKINNER, 'FOREWORD TO LIBER LUNAE'

Though not only are these incense utilized in this system, but also several different written '*words of power*' or evocations which are written upon parchment and burnt as incense themselves, though not for the purpose of scent. The evocations and words of power are transformed into summoning incense through the purification and alchemical transformation of fire, the element of Djinn. In this way, the energy circulates throughout the ritual chamber empowering it. This act represents the connection between the material and the spiritual worlds, where smoke dwells in the middle ground between that which is physical and spiritual. The words of power move about the ritual chamber in the form of smoke just as the Spirits, empowering the sacred magical space and becoming one with the Magician. As the Magician breathes in the empowered evocations, he transmutes them into vibrations by speaking the evocation, permeating the chamber with Intent and power. This is a form of Middle Eastern Spiritual Alchemy that has been utilized for millennia with great success, and has been employed herein.

The rites described within this manuscript are to be preformed solely by the Magician, though they can be easily altered to accommodate more practitioners. What I have continued to say throughout my works is, "Change Must Always Occur". This phrase can be applied to Magic in so many different ways, but overall what I am trying to convey is; Magic must be personalized. One must make magic their own, the rituals I present can and should be altered to the custom needs of the individual using them. This system must be made personal to be effective, don't perform '*my*' Magic, perform '*yours*'. Be free of the Traditional Magic Dogma. One must remember that any ritual they have ever read of or preformed was created by another Magician as '*they*' needed. When they came up with the ritual, they did it for themselves, not for the masses, and it worked for '*them*'. Therefore in a sense, it is their Magic. So, one must make these rituals their own by personalizing them with their own individualistic elements. Only when the Magician is behind his Magic, truly believing in it, truly '*feeling*' that the rite is 'right', will success be had.

The rituals presented here can be performed both inside as well as outside; it truly just depends on the situation. As an example, the Magician may both perform these rites under the stars in a cemetery, or inside a mausoleum within the same cemetery. Either way, the effect would be the same.

However, most of these rites will need to be held outside, due to the sheer size of the Magical Circles and Triangles of Arte.

The Lunate Script that is employed within this system is very powerful energetically. Its symbolic nature connects with the energy of the Waxing Crescent Moon and that of the night and darkness. The Lunate Script that is presented here was 'received' in the same timeframe as the Triangles and Circles of Arte as well as the Djinn Sigils, so you may wish to experiment using it first before you move on to customization, if you so choose. The symbols in the Lunate Script have many occult applications, and a complete explanation of their meaning and use will be released as its own work in the near future. Within the present work, they are used as letters and are given an English translation to be utilized within the Djinn sigils, on talismans, etc.

The Djinn listed within this grimoire are purely destructive by nature, and the Magician must use utmost caution when working with them. They are to be deployed when nothing less devastating will do. They are hate, pain and disease waiting to be released upon the world with a rage that is unmatched. If the 'Goetic' Spirits have a dark side, these Djinn are the embodiment of it. As stated this grimoire is a weapon, and does not make apologies for its existence. In fact, it is an 'ultimate weapon', to be unveiled and used when times are at their darkest. Those times are no longer on the horizon, they are here and are creeping in more little by little, day by day. The Black Magician who is in touch with his surroundings will know when to unleash this forbidden power; they will feel it deep within them…and recognize the feeling as rage. Each Warrior Magician will utilize this strength at different times, when the battle is at their door. There are no specific times to use this Magic, no Sabbats to attend, no nights to honor…it is to be used, when it is needed…at the time of War.

FROM BETWEEN THE ANGLES; CIRCLES & TRIANGLES OF THE ARTE MAGICAL

> *"The altars of violence and sacrifice: the temples of the Maya and Aztec magicians formed of trapezoids and sustained by the sacrificial blood of the chosen ones, the truncated pyramids upon which hearts were cut from living victims and held aloft and hot to Quetzalcoatl and Hapikern."*
> ANTON LaVEY

Magic is not *'Magical'*, it does not *'just happen'*, nor is it *'miraculous'*, it is a scientific system based on a process that we have yet to fully understand scientifically. I believe this is because we have yet to realize the totality of the base structure of the reality we are currently residing in. We have yet to understand all the rules of the *'Matrix'* of 'Consensual Reality' and therefore have yet to fully understand or utilize our personal place and power. Magic is the manipulation of personal energy to restructure the *'Consensual Reality Matrix'* to conform to the Intent of the Magician. As with all energy, Magic can be harnessed and directed, spirits and entities can be contacted and change can be made within the personal *'grid'* of the Magician.

There has always been a struggle of science vs. magic and which is 'true' and factual. This is ridiculous, they are the same. Nothing simply occurs, there is always a system, a process that must begin the *'miracle'*. As an example; if I were to sit in a room with an observer, chair facing chair, and suddenly move my left arm, it would appear to the observer that my arm moved with no outside cause, they would not see the hidden thought process in my brain that began the movement. Of course we know scientifically that there is a thought process that drives the functions of the human body, but if we lacked that scientific understanding, it would appear that my arm's movement was unconnected to any process other than its own sudden volition. This is Magic. We only see the outcome, though scientifically cannot explain it, yet. However, quantum physics has unraveled some of magic's mysteries and given us a scientific explanation for what was once thought of as *'miraculous'* such as in the example of sympathetic magic being discovered as entanglement or non-locality. If you take a piece of someone's hair and perform a magical baneful rite against them, they become sick, or whatever ill is willed onto them. Sympathetic magic has been practiced for centuries. Though now this is not magic, it is science because it has been somewhat explained by those who do not practice traditional Magic; largely the scientific community. Though even here science cannot yet explain why entanglement works, but we now 'scientifically', know that it does. The Magic has been correct all along, however it is now valid because it can be explained scientifically. As I said, this separation is ridiculous. It is my prediction that Magic will again one day be outlawed. Once the science behind magic can be verified and become factual, using a rite to inflict damage on another will not be seen any differently than hitting someone with a baseball bat. Books such as this will certainly be banned and seen as illegal weapons.

The approach this grimoire will take will implement a completely new foundation that has its roots set in Chaos Magic or *'Fringe Magic'* as I refer to it. Fringe Magic is not new; it is simply a category I have created to encompass scientific magic or magic that deals with dimensions, non-human intelligence and work that questions the basis of *'reality'*, and how to manipulate it. This can be classified as experimental magic if you will, teetering on the edge of the Abyss, or at least on the edge of what is magically socially acceptable. Up until about the last decade, any magical systems to be introduced to the public that did not stem from a hard structured Western Ceremonial Magical Order, were viewed with great discrimination. Only now are such concepts and ideas being looked upon with greater respect and interest. But even so, books such as this volume, or my last *"Volubilis Ex Chaosium"*, will still be scrutinized and rejected based on their un-conformity to the magical community's general appeal, acceptance or understanding. Simply because one embraces magic, does not mean one is open minded, intelligent or in-tune. I believe this discrimination is why *"The Necronomicon"* by Simon was placed in a background of Sumerian tradition, rather than being presented as a text of pure Chaos Magic, standing on its own. I believe the author felt it needed the legitimacy of a pre-existing culture and tradition to be accepted as a serious work in his time of publication. I have always thought the author should come out and present the manuscript for what it truly is; One of the first books of very powerful Chaos Magic. Regardless, this 'Experimental Magic' is still not held in the same upstanding way as magic that has its lineage to these traditional structured Orders, such as the O.T.O. and The Golden Dawn.

Of course Fringe Magic does encompass such literary works from authors and Magicians who have ventured forth into the *'empty spaces'*, such as H.P. Lovecraft, Carlos Castaneda, Pete Carroll, Frank G. Ripel, Michael Bertiaux, H.P. Blavatsky, Kenneth Grant and others who have been to the edge of creation and reality, and come back to write of it. They masterfully transform into words, experiences and concepts that are seemingly inde-scribable to those who have not walked the *'Spaces In-Between'* themselves, who have not known the *'Twilight of Being and Reality'*.

The practice of Magic dealing with the evocation of spirits, both benev-olent and baneful, has generally been centered around the Magic Circle and its counterpart; the Triangle of Arte. By using these key components, por-tals to other realms have been opened and contact with the spiritual entities has been achieved. Whether the magician were calling forth either Demons, Angels, or else, these tools have been implemented since time immemorial to commune with that which was *'beyond'*. I believe the key to opening these gateways between dimensions lies in angles, vibrations and direction of the Magician's personal energy and Intent.

H.P. Lovecraft has ever infused our idea of interdimensional travel and the opening of gateways with angles...angles beyond reason, or as he de-scribes in *"The Call Of Cthulhu"*,

"An angle which was acute, but behaved as if it were obtuse...".

Angles are the key to unlocking the dimensions, the key to traveling *'In-Between'* just as Keziah Mason used them to escape her prison cell in, *"The Dreams in the Witch House"*,

> *"...not even Cotton Mather could explain the curves and angles smeared on the grey stone walls with some red, sticky fluid."...* *"She had told Judge Hathorne of lines and curves that could be made to point out directions leading through the walls of space to other spaces beyond, and had implied that such lines and curves were frequently used at certain midnight meetings in the dark valley of the white stone beyond Meadow Hill and on the unpeopled island in the river"*
>
> H.P. LOVECRAFT,
> 'THE DREAMS IN THE WITCH HOUSE', 1933

Within angles, there is energy known as 'Static Energy' that is tightly compressed as a spring. It is much as a twig being squeezed between two fingers, that begins to bend from the pressure, but not yet break. This energy is ready to be released and directed under the right conditions. If the correct angles are utilized in conjunction with the correct vocal vibrations, the angles are *'snapped'*, and the static energy released, thus opening doors to other dimensions that are unlocked for travel, both to and from another point, an example is the evocation of Yog~Sothoth given in *"Volubilis Ex Chaosium"* *(As will be discussed)*. Within the 'correct' angles, doorways between realms can, will, and have opened. Oftentimes at this juncture between dimensions, lie guardians or guides that one must either master or follow, such as Choronzon, Papa Legba, Nyarlathotep, etc., depending on which system of magic is being utilized. Concerning entities and traveling between the planes, H.P. Lovecraft again writes,

> *"...his sober theory (was) that a man might - given mathematical knowledge admittedly beyond all likelihood of human acquirement - step deliberately from the earth to any other celestial body which might lie at one of an infinity of specific points in the cosmic pattern. Such a step, he said, would require only two stages; first, a passage out of the three-dimensional sphere*

*we know, and second, a passage back to the three-dimensional sphere at another point, perhaps one of infinite remoteness. That this could be accomplished without loss of life was in many cases conceivable. Any being from any part of three-dimensional space could probably survive in the fourth dimension; and its survival of the second stage would depend upon what alien part of three-dimensional space it might select for its re-entry. Denizens of some planets might be able to live on certain others - even planets belonging to other galaxies, or to similar dimensional phases of other space-time continua - though of course there must be vast numbers of mutually uninhabitable even though mathematically juxtaposed bodies or zones of space. It was also possible that the inhabitants of a given dimensional realm could survive entry to many unknown and incomprehensible realms of additional or indefinitely multiplied dimensions - be they within or outside the given space-time continuum - and that the converse would be likewise true. This was a matter for speculation, though one could be fairly certain that the type of mutation involved in a passage from any given dimensional plane to the next higher one would not be destructive of biological integrity as we understand it...**Professor Upham especially liked his demonstration of the kinship of higher mathematics to certain phases of magical lore transmitted down the ages from an ineffable antiquity - human or pre-human - whose knowledge of the cosmos and its laws was greater than ours.***"*

H.P. LOVECRAFT, *"DREAMS IN THE WITCH HOUSE"*

It has been known for some time that within angles there is hidden power waiting to be released. As well, it has also been studied, that angles have a profound effect upon the human mind, its perceptions and emotions.

"Angles are space-planes that provoke anxiety...that is, those not harmonious with natural visual orientation, will engender aberrant behavior. Exceptions occur where a sort of reverse polarity exists in a creature: extreme mental imbalance or perversity, or perhaps even extreme rationality and awareness."

ANTON LaVEY

Though not only is the human mind altered in such a way, but also the ability to be effected on an overall scale spiritually via dimensional shifts of time and space. Anton LaVey's Law of the Trapezoid reads as follows,

"All obtuse angles are magically harmful to those unaware of this property. The same angles are beneficial, stimulating and energizing to those who are magically sensitive to them"
ANTON LaVEY

LaVey comments on his law,

"If the Law of the Trapezoid is known, recognized when applicable, and either heeded or utilized, it will save much hardship and tragedy, while still serving as a catalyst for change. Like fire, its powers are two-fold, depending on how it is applied. Like the sun, its powers are two-fold, depending on whether a thing is growing, grown, or dying. And like the first crystalline fusion of atoms, it will be the beginning and the end, the Alpha and Omega of all matter. Avert your gaze from the pyramids and look to the trapezoid, and you shall be moved."
ANTON LaVEY

An interesting commentary from a reputable source on LaVey's Law,

"What exactly happens when an individual enters an angular environment ? It is very apparent that a polarity is produced within the individual. This is in essence what the 'Law of the Trapezoid' describes. Some are attracted to the environment and others are repelled. Along with attraction comes mental imagery that tries to encompass infinite concepts. Those who are repelled go to the opposite with imagery that has a profound morbid aspect connected to it. Feelings of impending death on a individual and species wide scale, theirs is a finite image. These are generalizations; I have seen extremes with both polarities.

The bottom line is that there is an effect produced, no one really understands the actual nature of the effects, nor its boundaries, we will find out.

"*Most certainly each individual has felt the effects of an angular environment. Many symbols incorporate angular features into their motif, and most certainly we have all felt moved by particular music forms in a manner falling into the above description of what happens in an angular environment. Haunted house phenomena is most common in homes that have many angular shapes both inside and out.* **Angles produce the 'Command To Look'**, *which then motivates into a polarity which can be predictable. The ability to unlock the secret of the angles will allow a more precise refining of (their) exhilarating -and thus inspiring- properties...*"

R. WHITAKER, SETIAN PRIEST,
'THE LAW OF THE TRAPAZOID.'

The particular 'Triangles of Arte' being presented here are designed to keep the mind fluctuating, never resting on one plane, but between them. Their design encompasses both two dimensional and three dimensional space simultaneously, conjoined into one form that is occupying neither space at any one given moment. It is in this twilight, this constant flux, which resides '*between the angles*', that an entity may cross the dimensional boundary and enter our world or ritual space where communication is achieved. This system utilizes a philosophy which incorporates new concepts for the Triangles of Arte as well as the Magical Circles, and should not be considered tied to the "*Goetia*", but seen as its own work, with its own set of guidelines and applications.

The 'Triangles' are not only employed for ritual work, but are also very useful in meditation when working with a specific Djinn. These Triangles not only offer a gateway for the spiritual entity into our 'realm', but also provide a gateway for the Magicians mind to enter into theirs. This method was utilized for the construction of the Djinn Sigils and Lunate Script presented within. One will notice that when viewing the 'Triangles' that it is difficult to look away, this is the natural power that lies within the designs themselves that draws one in, having a hypnotic effect on the viewer, and again the words echo, "**Angles produce the 'Command To Look'**. This attraction is not a negative effect, the Magician should allow himself to be drawn into the angles and become open to their energies.

This system is powered by the Magician/Operator. He is the central force the rite is based around. Without the power of the Operator, the Circles and Triangles are simply designs upon the ground. Yes, still holding power as described, but not what is required to open the doorways 'In-Between', they must be charged with the energy of the Magician. When the angles are 'snapped', and the energy released, it opens a rift in the 'Consensual Reality Matrix' allowing for the Magician to project his Intent. This also includes interaction between Organic and In-Organic entities, i.e., between the Magician and the Djinn in this case. Obviously this technology can and should be applied to other workings outside of this system.

There are three Triangles of Arte that are employed within this system which the Magician will utilize when summoning Djinn. Each has a design that concentrates the flow of static energy within the angles, making them a powerful vortex, or portal when activated. This allows for the Djinn to cross through the doorway of '*The Spaces In-Between (the angles)*', and into the ritual space of the Magician, where the intended interaction may occur. The Triangles can be seen as machines or circuit boards that require energy to be activated. Likewise the Circles are generators that amplify and enhance the collected personal energy of the Magician allowing him to transfer that energy into the Triangle, in effect 'turning it on'. It will take time to correctly lay out the Circle and Triangle configurations, but it must be remembered that Magic should not be seen as a chore, but an embracement of godhood. Take the time, it is sacred. When drawing out the Triangles, do not let your mind wander to what you will do after the rite, what you are doing next week with friends, or other subjects that divert your energy away from the task at hand. Instead, one must concentrate on the rite to be preformed, the desired results, and subjects related to the work. The longer one spends channeling this imagery and energy into the creation of the Magical Circles and Triangles, the more empowered the configurations become, thus the more energized the rite itself becomes.

The Magical Circles employed are as the Triangles, also having a specific function. Though unlike the Triangles which are designed to open rifts, the

Circles are designed to amplify and encompass the Magician's stored personal energy so that it may be transferred into the Triangles, igniting them with raw energy in preparation of being activated.

The basic concept of these Triangles and Circles is very M.C. Escher esque. They have angles, planes and perspectives that cannot exist simultaneously with one another in a three dimensional world, as solidly as they appear in print. This is the Magic of Escher's artwork, he too saw and understood that indeed, *'Angles produce the command to look'*, and that people are drawn to them for some, yet unknown reason. I personally believe the reason to be found within our primal instincts. It is an instilled knowledge we of today are vaguely aware of, underneath all of our conscious thoughts and organizations based on reason and rationality. Indeed, it is an unspoken or consciously known truth with the very absence of reason, of why or how, that extends its reach deeper than any conventional understanding of the taught, neatly packaged and explained universe. Without knowing why, we understand angles contain energy and are portals to places *'other'*.

The concept of these Triangles and Circles further push the ideals of what is conventionally thought of as workable or 'acceptable' vehicles or instruments of the Arte Magical. Never before has this dimensional technology been introduced into the Magical community in such a direct fashion. However, I have found traces of it in Frederick Hockley's work, such as in *"The Complete Book of Magic Science"* as well as in *"Experimentum"*, though these works have been copied from other pre-existing grimoires and manuscripts and did not originate from Hockley's own hand. The importance of angles can also be seen in Francis Bacon's grimoire *"De Nigromancia"*, which interestingly deals with the conjuration of Wraiths, an unconventional entity to summon in general, which indeed fits well into the family of inter-dimensional, in-organic intelligences. The Triangles of Arte presented here are true energetic portals, reaching through time and space to provide passage into our realm of existence so that contact with In-Organic entities may be achieved. They are a Magical Engine waiting to be activated...

THE FIRST TRIANGLE contains both two and three dimensional perspectives simultaneously. The angles of the configuration are all contrived from three, two dimensional squares turned point facing down, spread out in the formation of an inverted isosceles triangle. This grouped triangle of squares is joined together by a line connecting all three in the apex of each squares origin of angles. Additionally, two more lines are directed outward from the bottom squares apex of angles through the squares juncture of planes to an exact point where they change course sharply converging at the center point above the lower central square. Now when viewing the total design these second set of angles create the perspective of the top of a three dimensional cube. This can be seen by way of the lower squares apex of angles supporting two triangular, partial faces of the cube. When the top of the three dimensional cube perspective converges with the lines connecting the three two dimensional squares, the basis of two natural pentagrams emerge that are neither two, nor three dimensional in perspective, but both as their lines of existence are formed from both two and three dimensional planes. When viewing the total image or Triangle, the mind cannot rest upon one perspective alone, shifting from a two dimensional view, to a three dimensional view, and then impossibly…to both at once… then shifting again.

THE SECOND TRIANGLE is of a simpler design, though again sharing both a two and three dimensional perspective or space as the above described Triangle. This Triangle consists of three elongated two dimensional isosceles triangles that are all connected by the points of their base, creating an equilateral triangle in the center connecting all three. This formed two dimensional equilateral triangle is also the point of the three dimensional pentagram that is angled at such a way as to create the perspective of a three dimensional downward slanting plane intersecting with the two dimensional plane, the downward point/center of the isosceles triangle like the pentagrams in the first Triangle share both a two and three dimensional space simultaneously.

THE THIRD TRIANGLE is much more complex than the second, consisting of six conjoined, reversed and mirrored triangles. The best way to describe this Triangle would be to split it in half, top to bottom. When viewing the Triangle, the left side consists of three triangles, one large isosceles on its side, apex pointed 'to the right side'. Overlaid symmetrically within its structure is another slightly smaller isosceles triangle, also on its side with its apex pointing to the right side like the larger triangle it is overlaid upon, though its base extends out past the base of the larger triangle it rests upon. Resting on top of the larger triangle lays yet another isosceles triangle, though its apex is facing the left or opposite direction and extents no farther than the base of the large triangle lying flush to its left side. The right side of the main Triangle is configured in the same way, though the apex of the large triangle overlaps the apex of the large triangle on the right side, to the point of touching the apex of the smaller imbedded triangle. Now the main Triangle is joined by way of both large triangles overlapping and touching the apexes of the opposite smaller imbedded triangles. And as on the left side of the main Triangle, there is one smaller isosceles triangle to be positioned on the bottom of the right larger isosceles triangle, its apex (like its mirrored twin) extending no farther than the base of the larger isosceles triangle. As with the first two Triangles, once the mind has shifted into a relaxed state, dimension within the Triangles begin to unfold. This particular gateway becomes an open box like structure that is impossible to construct on the physical plane, as some have attempted to construct it with no success.

THE FIRST CIRCLE Rests in an angular cradle of compressed static energy, having yet another circle partially surround it. Its design focuses on having a continuous stream of Universal energy run through the Magician while combining with his own within the Circle. 'Lunate Script' is inscribed within the space between the two concentric circles and in various angles where space is provided.

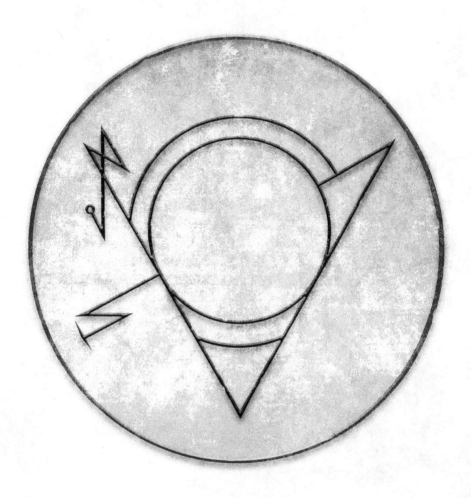

THE SECOND CIRCLE is also very angular; having four intertwined isosceles offset triangles, equally run through two oine circle. Rather than drawing in energy, the function of this Circle is to enhance the Magician's own stored energy. 'Lunate Script' may be added between the circle and angles where space is provided.

THE THIRD CIRCLE is similar to the second, in that it too is designed to amplify the Magician's own energy. It consists of two concentric circles that are embraced by two inward facing crescent moons to each side. On the top and bottom of the circle are two isosceles triangles with a bowed base to match the curve of the main circle.

Smokeless Fire

Intent and Vibration

The use of incantations, evocations, invocations and the like, all have the base science of vibrating the Intent, or energy of the Magician into the Magician's subjective 'reality', causing the desired change to occur. This is also used when calling upon a particular entity; names have power because they are a specific vibration sequence that is connected to the entity being called forth. An entities name is as powerful and connected to it as its magical seal or sigil,

"The essential character of things and of men resides in their names. Therefore to know a name is to be privy to the secret of its owner's being, and master of his fate. The members of many primitive tribes have two names, one for public use, the other jealously concealed, known only to the man who bears it."..."To know the name of a man is to exercise power over him alone; to know the name of a higher, supernatural being is to dominate the entire province over which that being presides. The more such names a magician has garnered, the greater the number of spirits that are subject to his call and command. This simple theory is at the bottom of the magic which operates through the mystical names and words that are believed to control the forces which in turn control our world. The spirits guarded their names as jealously as ever did a primitive tribe."

JOSHUA TRACHTENBERG,
'JEWISH MAGIC AND SUPERSTITION',1939

THE BOOK OF SMOKELESS FIRE

Though, it is not the name itself that is important, but the names particular vibration into reality that is. Sound and vibration are key in this system to excite and release the static energy that is built up within the entwined angles that compose the Triangles of Arte. Sound has always been defined as a wave, and while true, this term does not accurately describe how sound truly behaves. Sound waves exist as variations of pressure in a medium such as air. They are created by the vibration of an object, which causes the molecules within the air surrounding it to vibrate. The vibrating air then causes the human eardrum to vibrate, which the brain interprets as sound. Sound is an expanding bubble made up of one existing connected wave, it is vibration composed of pure energy. The energy excites the molecules around it causing them in turn to vibrate, starting a chain reaction to occur until the molecules have lost all of their excitement the further away they get from the source, resulting in 'silence'.

The audio pressures or vibrations upon the Triangles of Arte in conjunction with the personal energy of the Magician, excite the compacted static energy within the angles until an apex is reached and the energy released, much as in sexual orgasm. Here lies the process of frustration, excitation and release. As stated this type of hyper-sexual frustration is especially seen within the polygon of the trapezoid, unable to connect with its missing counterpart (the triangle) creating union, and streamlining the flow of energy contained within.

Contrary to popular belief, there are no exact correct words of power to be said in a rite. All that is important is that the Magician fully infuse their words with emotion and Intent. When this is done, the Magician imprints his Intent onto and into the Consensual Reality Matrix and changes the coding, or structure for an outcome that was personally desired and would not normally come to pass. Deep vibrations of Magical Intent make more of an impact and get better results as the energy is imprinted more deeply onto 'reality'. Though this varies as there are times a Magician's Intent can be so strong that their words can be whispered and still have devastating effect.

> "It is not known to me whether any of my readers have witnessed
> any kind of magical ceremony, or heard an invocation recited
> by a skilled practitioner – though I should say few have. The
> tone always adopted is one which will yield the maximum of

vibration. For many students a deep intoning, or a humming, is one which vibrates the most."
Israel Regardie,
'Foundations of Practical Magic'

An example of the use of pure emotional vibration can be seen in grimoires such as , *"Tuba Veneris: Libellus Veneri Nigro Sacer"* that use barbarous words of power. The words themselves have no meaning, they are solely there to be used as a vibrational vehicle upon which the Magician's Intent travels. In such rites, pure vibration and intent is all that is needed to accomplish the ritual being performed.

> *"Long lists of divine names and words of Power, sometimes called **Barbarous Words of Power, were recited in the form of litanies**. In the Clavicle of Solomon revealed to Ptolemy we find the instruction that once **the magician had recited all these names with the utmost devotion** one was advised: "Heare let the maiesty of god cum in." The implication is that by calling upon the hierarchy of divine names, the operator was invoking those specific aspects of God's holy power and focusing it into the magic circle and thus bringing it into the person therein."*
> William Kiesel,
> 'Magic Circles in the Grimoire Tradition'.

It is clear that even though the Forces being called forth in this example originate in Order, the base science is the same; a pattern of vibration is laid down as the vehicle, while the emotional Intent is the passenger. Another example of this can be seen in Lovecraft's works. His use of seemingly unpronounceable names for the Old Ones and their evocations is well known. He has maximized the vibrational science so contact is more easily made between intelligences. I have featured his barbarous words in the Yog~Sothoth evocation within *"Volubilis Ex Chaosium"*,

> *"I call out to,*
> *and into,*
> *the primordial absolute chaos of the darkened abyss,*

I call to the endless void of absolute silent black,
that lies in the deep waters of cold truth,
I call to you,
to bring 'Him' forth...
I call to the All~In~One And One~In~All,
the all seeing one who dwells in the negative light of cold understanding,
I call you Beyond One,
into this dark Temple to become the Gate,
I Call Yog~Sothoth !
I Call The Gate Keeper !
Come Forth Yog~Sothoth !"

"Yog~Sothoth knows the Gate,
Yog~Sothoth is the Key and Guardian of the Gate !
Yog~Sothoth you are now called forth to take form as the Trinity Of
Triangles,
to manifest as the Three~In~Nine and Become the Triangles,
so that I may open Your Gates and summon forth the Old Ones,
so I may answer Their call,
and so They may answer mine !
Yog~Sothoth I call you to manifest as the Trinity Of Triangles,
Yog~Sothoth become the Gateway Between ! Yog~Sothoth Become !
N'gai ~ n'gha'ghaa ~ bugg-shoggog ~ y'hah; Yog-Sothoth ~ Yog-Sothoth...
N'gai ~ n'gha'ghaa ~ bugg-shoggog ~ y'hah; Yog-Sothoth ~ Yog-Sothoth...
N'gai ~ n'gha'ghaa ~ bugg-shoggog ~ y'hah; Yog-Sothoth ~ Yog-Sothoth...

Ygnaiih ~ Ygniih ~ Thflthkh'ngha ~ Yog-Sothoth,
Y'bthnk ~ H'ehye ~ N'grkdl'lh...
Ygnaiih ~ Ygniih ~ Thflthkh'ngha ~ Yog-Sothoth,
Y'bthnk ~ H'ehye ~ N'grkdl'lh...
Ygnaiih ~ Ygniih ~ Thflthkh'ngha ~ Yog-Sothoth,
Y'bthnk ~ H'ehye ~ N'grkdl'lh...

Yi-nash-Yog-Sothoth-he-lgeb-fi-throdog Yah !
Yi-nash-Yog-Sothoth-he-lgeb-fi-throdog Yah !
Yi-nash-Yog-Sothoth-he-lgeb-fi-throdog Yah !"

Let The Gateway Be Opened!

Again, we see such seemingly random compilations of letters also within the Enochian Magical System, where the names of the Angels and such are based on a vocal system that is vibrated such as the Enochian Keys or Calls. Also in the Enochian system we see these vocal vibrations being used in conjunction with the Sigil dei Emeth, or the Sigil of Truth which contains many angles of frustration containing static energy. And, in the controversial *"Tuba Veneris: Libellus Veneri Nigro Sacer"* of the 16th century, also said to also be of John Dee's hand, we see again the use of barbarous words in the invocations given for the Spirits. Here is an example of the invocation given for the Spirit Mogarip,

> *"Mogarip! Mogarip! Mogarip!*
> *Hamka Temach Algazoth Syrath*
> *Amilgos Murzocka Imgat*
> *Alaja Amgustaroth Horim Suhaja*
> *Mogarip! Mogarip! Mogarip!*

As well, within the traditional Voodoo/Vodoun systems the heavy vibration of drums is utilized to excite and transmit the emotion of the masses to the Lwa they are attempting to contact. An amazing first hand account of a Vodoun rite which incorporated the use of drums, is given by Richard Loederer in his book *"Voodoo Fire in Haiti"* published in 1935,

> *"As we rode through the night, the drums were beating again – but with a new rhythm that I had never heard before. I was keyed up to a pitch of perspiring excitement, fearing what was to come and yet unwilling to turn back. We were about to participate in a monstrous performance, an orgy which not one white man in a million has ever seen. Tonight was a Voodoo Fire, and we were to be present"…"The path climbed upward amongst the jagged hills. Below us lay the town and, far off, the sea, glittering in the moonlight. It was a warm night, yet the pale rays of the moon cast a chill aura of malignant evil over the whole scene. We rode through a cemetery where the whitewashed tombstones flitted*

past like serried ranks of ghosts, then the dark shape of trees rose up again on either side, stretching their gnarled branches in our way. And all the while the hollow booming of the drums rang in our ears; now nearer, now further, rising and falling in subtle cadences. Often it seemed as if the sound were no more than half a mile away and then it faded into a distant throb. Strange... the nearer we approached, the fainter it became. But it never died completely away nor ever varied its rhythm. There were two distinct phases in the refrain. **First the short, staccato: Tom-ti-ti-tom...luring and enticing; then the surging, heavy Boom-boom, threatening and compelling. The drums were calling, they drugged the will until all resistance died. I realized with impotent horror that it was impossible to turn back; the power of the drums was too great.**"

RICHARD LOEDERER

One can clearly see the importance of the Vodoun drum and the atmosphere it creates to literally draw in all who hear it and project their energy onto the Lwa they are attempting to contact. The drums are central to tapping into the human psyche and pulling out its primal nature to be utilized as a power source for contacting human and non-human entities. I also find it interesting that this first hand account reads very much like that of Lovecraft's sequence *"Nyarlathotep"* published in 1921, where the main character is compelled against his will into a vast swirling vortex of destruction and death, driven by the mad sound of beating drums and shrill terrifying flutes,

*"***My own column was sucked toward the open country,** *and presently felt a chill which was not of the hot autumn; for as we stalked out of the dark moor, we beheld around us the hellish moon-glitter of evil snows. Trackless, inexplicable snows, swept asunder in one direction only, where lay a gulf all the blacker for its glittering walls.* **The column seemed very thin indeed as it plodded dreamily into the gulf**"..."*As if beckoned by those who had gone before, I half floated between the titanic snowdrifts, quivering and afraid, into the sightless vortex of the unimaginable.*"..."*And through this revolting graveyard*

of the universe **the muffled, maddening beating of drums, and thin, monotonous whine of blasphemous flutes** *from inconceivable, unlighted chambers beyond Time;* **the detestable pounding and piping** *whereunto dance slowly, awkwardly, and absurdly the gigantic, tenebrous ultimate gods – the blind, voiceless, mindless gargoyles whose soul is Nyarlathotep."*

H.P. LOVECRAFT

There is a science to opening the Gateways of the 'In-Between'; it is founded in three base principles; the use and release of static energy within angles, the Intent of the Magician, and the Vibration to imprint the Magician's Intent upon the Consensual Reality Matrix. With these tools, all is possible.

SmokelessFire

REQUIRED RITUAL TOOLS

agical tools vary greatly from one system to another, they are not the main focus of a rite, but a vital part of it. They are the means through which the Magician manipulates and communes with the spatial energy of the *'Consensual Reality Matrix'*. It is through these vital elements that the Magician shapes reality around him. Magical tools are energetic pieces of the whole, which contain specific energetic properties that correspond to one another, the Magician and to the magical rite itself, thus empowering it. They are designed as well, to draw out energy from the Magician to be focused on a specific magical task.

This system has few magical tools employed, it is powerfully simple, and it focuses on the Magician being the magical energy source for the rites involved. The tools that are utilized, are used for evocation, direction/command and protection, and are drawn from ancient magical praxis. They are the simple key elements that help provide and manipulate the power of the Black Magician to the Magical Engine that is the Triangle of Arte.

Magical tools have also been seen as beneficial visual props, they help to put the Magician into the correct state of mind in order to unlock and fully utilize the hidden energy forces that are already at his command, that lie dormant until stimulated/activated.

This system utilizes a bit of both of those practices, combining them in a way that is potent magically as well as visually, emerging the Magician into the deep needed state of mind to perform the task at hand. The magical tools in combination with the incense, words of power, Circle and Triangle of Arte, create the ideal gathering of energy. These elements set and prepare the atmosphere for the Magician to open the passageway *'Between the Spaces'*, allowing for interaction to occur between intelligences, be they spiritual, alien, or other.

CHALK/FLOUR/CRUSHED EGGSHELLS: Chalk, flour and crushed eggshells are used in this system to layout the Magical Circles and Triangles of Arte. The choice of material is left to the Magician, however one should consider where the ritual is to be held when deciding, as some materials may be applied better than the others.

BRASS LAMP/INCENSE DISH: Staying close to tradition, I have found that using an Arabic brass lamp for an incense burner adds a lot visually to the ritual. However any brass incense holder will work. The lamp is not specifically needed, and can be considered a magical prop, though as stated such props can be beneficial to the Magician. A second brass incense dish is also needed for the Magician to burn the Words of Power, Sigils and Evocations. The lamp and dish can be inscribed with Lunate Script to empower them.

STRIPS OF PARCHMENT PAPER: Cut strips of parchment paper is used to inscribe Sigils, Evocations and Words of Power onto. These are burnt before, during and after a rite.

BLACKTHORN/EBONY/OAK SCEPTER: A scepter of blackthorn, ebony or oak is used, as these particular woods hold magical qualities that are in tune with the darker chthonic aspects of magic, namely death and the underworld and the gateways between. The scepter can be inscribed with Lunate Script to empower it.

MAGICAL SWORD: A sword is used in this system as a show of strength and authority. Because these Djinn carry out the Magician's command does not mean that they don't wish to tear him apart as well. These entities are dangerous and wish all humanity pain and death, the Magician is no exception. However, they will be guided by a Black Magician as they are pleased at any opportunity to spread disease and death, especially if they know that the Magician will call them forth again. Djinn can be hurt, possibly killed with ONE strike of a sword, any additional strikes will render the Djinn immune to attack and it will surely be upon you. However, the sword truly is utilized as a representation to the Djinn that the Black Magician is a warrior as they are, and that he will fight. It is a show of personal strength, rather than a threat. It is there to establish a silent respect between two warriors that may not be on the same side, though forge a truce to accomplish similar goals.

BLOOD: This has been discussed.

SACRIFICIAL BOWL: A sacrificial bowl is used to contain the blood spilt during ritual. It is not to be used for any other purpose, and kept wrapped in a black silk cloth when not in use. To empower it further, Lunate Script is employed.

This assortment of magical instruments is all that is needed in this system. These tools all have an important role, however, the power source behind all this occult science, lies within the Black Magician. There are magical engines within this system such as the three Triangles and Circles of Arte , though it is the Black Magician that is the 'Key', the core and central magical engine that drives all else forth. It is with the use of these magical tools that the Magician raises and directs the needed energy to complete the rite. Of course as stated, this system must be personalized to be effective, therefore the Magician must add their own elements into the system where they feel they are needed.

LUNATE SCRIPT

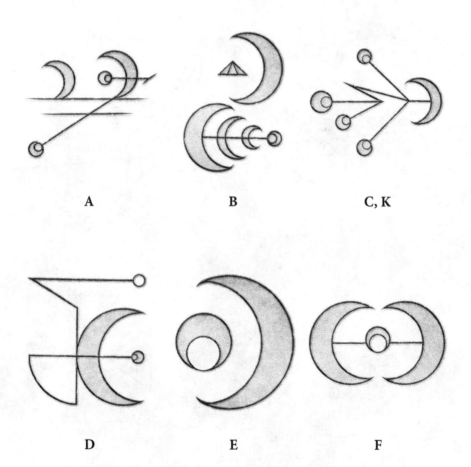

A   B   C, K

D   E   F

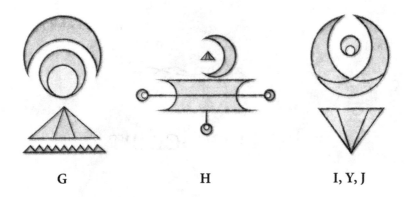

G   H   I, Y, J

L   M

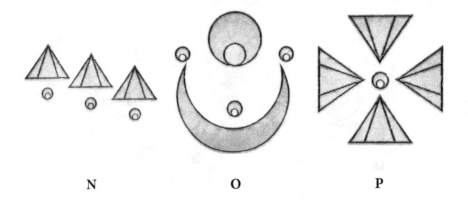

N   O   P

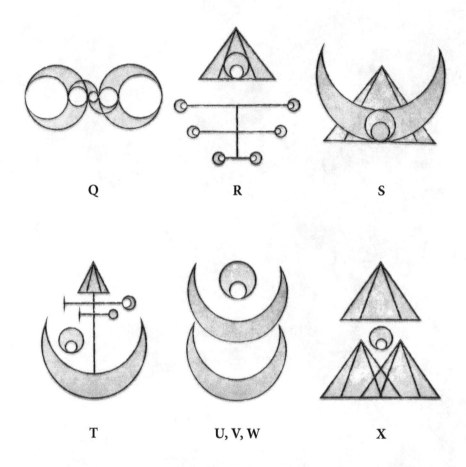

Q   R   S

T   U, V, W   X

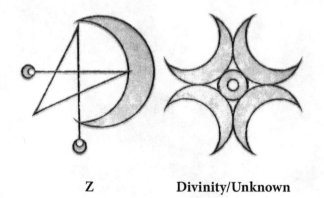

Z   Divinity/Unknown

BOOK II

SUMMONING THE INFERNAL DJINN

ALIGNING WITH TRUE CHAOS

his rite is designed to align or more accurately, re-align the Magician's energy to that of the true Chaos current that flows through all who are of the LHP. This rite is designed to connect the Magician with the pure Black Snake Current of Chaos. Here the manifested form of Chaos is seen and worked with as a Blackened Serpent, representing the true form of Chaos. This rite does not need to be preformed immediately before evoking the Djinn, but is recommended to help cultivate energy within the Magician. This ritual has been adapted from a Nyarlathorep working, though there is little difference between Nyarlathotep as a face of Chaos and Chaos itself, and so readily applies within this system.

This working is to be held outside at dusk where it is quiet and you will not be disturbed. You will need a red candle and small bowl of consecrated water. Find 'Your Place' by walking the area and 'feeling' which specific spot will be suitable for your work. It could take time, but do not rush this process, it is very important to locate the correct area upon the earth which you will perform your rite.

Once you have found your proper work space, create a circle upon the Earth nine feet in diameter out of whatever natural material may be presently available, such as rocks or branches from nearby foliage. Pour the consecrated water into a clean bowl (if not already there), and stand outside the circle with it before you, state clearly with intention,

> "Let this circle of Art be empowered and cleansed by
> the shadows of these dark waters of the In-Between"

Sprinkle the sacred water in the closed circle with your first and middle fingers, covering its entirety, though being careful to reserve some. Once done, place your fingers upon your forehead where your third spiritual eye rests and state,

> "Let this vessel of flesh be cleansed and prepared
> for the sinister Spirit of the Blackened Snake that
> winds His way ever through this reality"

Walk into the circle of Art and sit down cross legged, slow your pulse and breathe deep. Light the red candle and place it just inside the edge of the circle directly in front of you, making sure to place the sacred water bowl to the left of it, and state,

> "Black flame of Chaos eternal, ignite the fires
> in the realms of Twilight and permit passage
> into this world from Spaces In-Between"

Dig down and put a small amount of top soil in the palm of each of your hands, resting them face up upon your knees, connect with the Earth and the Air. Close your eyes and meditate, calm yourself clearing your mind of all internal dialogue. Visualize a black hole about 6"in. in diameter just below the center of your chest, where your solar plexus is located. Visualize you are but a shell – empty, and that hole leads to your inside. Now visualize a sinister black snake directly facing you about 6'ft. in front of the circle of Art. Lock eyes with the serpent, 'see' it and connect with it – invite it in, for it is Chaos manifest. Watch as the snake slithers silently toward you, the circle is not there to keep it out, but to concentrate energy into a purified area, the blackened serpent has no trouble crossing the boundary that divides you. It stops inches from you and raises its head up to the level of the hole that resides within you, and you see its head enter your body, feel the black scales sliding into you. As it enters you, it is coiling itself under the hole you have envisioned. Feel the entire serpent coiled up within you, filling your chest cavity. Feel its weight and strength.

When it has finished and is still, feel it growing in strength, pulsating. it draws strength from you in waves, getting stronger then leveling out, getting stronger then leveling out, until you can hold the Serpent back no more. As it has nearly drained you of all energy, it bursts forth from you, shooting its strength throughout all your limbs, filling your empty shell with His unworldly Black strength. As the serpent leaves your body it sheds its skin, leaving its essence to ever reside within. See the Black current flowing through you, completely filling you. Visualize that abundant energy flow from the hole of its exit begin to cover your body. See it expand out across your chest in all directions, quickly flowing over your stomach, around and up your back, out and down each leg through your feet, over your shoulders and down each arm, through your hands and fingers, feel it race up your neck, over your face and through your hair. Open your mouth and drink it in – it has washed over and through you. You are now cleansed and filled with the power and essence of the Blacked Serpent of Chaos…Open your eyes. You have now the primal force of darkness forever within.

This meditation is very powerful, and leaves one 'seeing' the world in a different way than before it began. It is recommended that this rite be done every three months to reenergize and align your energy with the Black current of Chaos.

The Conjuration Of The Eternal Black Flame

"Fire, in all things, and through all things, comes and goes away bright; it is in all things bright, and at the same time occult and unknown."

Dionysius

ire is a violent force of elemental energy, it destroys, and yet from the scorched Earth it brings forth new life. Fire is transition; it is a change in a drastic and often instant manner, creating new form from old. It is Alchemical in both its essence and action, existent upon the physical plane, yet holding properties that are ethereal as the Spirits themselves. The Black Magician who is in tune with his environment is able to feel these occult essences, and have for aeons worshiped and given honor to this 'Spirit of Fire' that they instinctively are aware of.

The Conjuration of the Eternal Black Flame/The Conjuration of Fire presented here takes on a different meaning than what is normally associated with the rite. The Conjuration of Fire within the *"Goetia"* is designed to threaten Demons with an ever increasing degree of pain and wrath, if they do not appear to the Magician when first called. This rite is horrendous. The first call is made, if no response is detected, a second conjuration is given. At this point if still no response by the Demon, the threats begin to make themselves known. First the 'Constraint' is given threatening to,

"...curse and deprive you (the Demon), from all your office, Joy &
place, and binde you in the depth of ye Bottomless pit There to
remaine unto the day of the last Judgement, and I will bind you
into Eternal fire & into the lake of fire and Brimstone, unless you
come forthwith and appeare heere before this Circle to doe my
will in all things."

"The Lesser Key of Solomon',
Edited by Joseph Peterson

After reading this, is it any wonder why the Demons would despise the Judeo/Christian Magician, and why he would need protection from them ? The conjuration almost reads like a spoiled child throwing a fit, demanding he get his way *'or else'*. Following the 'Constraint', there remains 'The Invocation of the King', followed by 'The General Curse', followed by 'The Conjuration of Fire', ending with 'The Curse'. Each round of threats become more degrading and promise more pain. Though the Djinn within this system differ from the Demons of the Goetia, they are also dangerous and would gladly tear the Magician apart, they are not to be threatened or disrespected, it is not the way to work with them and will yield negative results, not to mention gain enemies the Magician surly would not desire...nor have for long.

There is a very fine balance of power between the Black Magician and the Djinn, it is more of a partnership or silent understanding between the two, than it is a master and servant relationship. The Magician conjures them to destroy; they come because they enjoy inflicting great pain upon humanity. The Magician is human; they overlook this as they wish to be called again for the opportunity to be directed at new targets. However, if they are disrespected, there really are no safeguards that can hold them at bay; this is why these rites must be undertaken with such great caution. Of course the sword implemented does offer some protection, though very little. Imagine if you will, fighting an incredibly malicious, interdimensional, shape-shifting and sometimes invisible entity that is as old as time, that has seventy-one angry brothers and sisters...only armed with a sword. It's possible the Magician could get lucky, but it's not likely. The sword is a representation to the Djinn, that the Black Magician is a warrior as they are, and that he will fight. It is a show of strength. Showing weakness and fear in this situation will only result in ruin.

The rite described here has a completely different aim than the Goetic 'Conjuration of Fire', it is not used to threaten the Djinn, but to raise the essence of the 'Eternal Black Flame' that lies in the Darkness of True Chaos. Fire is the elemental essence of Djinn, it flows as blood through their veins, it is a purifying ethereal flame which gives off no smoke. Fire destroys, but also cleanses, these Djinn are of that essence, and that is why they are being set loose with the creation of this tome; to cleanse and prepare the Earth for new growth.

As the Aligning rite already described harmonizes the Magician with the true force of Chaos, the intention here is to conjure and give honor and respect to 'The Eternal Black Flame' that is not only the pure essence of the Djinn, but also of all those true born of Chaos. By performing the 'Aligning Ritual' with 'The Conjuration of the Eternal Black Flame' (not at once), the Magician increases his spiritual personal energy by connecting to the 'source' of both 'True Chaos' and that of 'The Eternal Black Flame'. True Chaos is the *body*, while the Eternal Black Flame is the *core*, the *blood* and *wisdom* that flows within.

This rite is to be performed at night under the stars, preferably in a desert like area where the Magician will not be disturbed. The Triangle of Arte employed is designed to concentrate the essence of 'The Eternal Black Flame', this is accomplished by the use of 'The Infernal Trapezoid'. Within the Triangle of Arte, a trapezoid is incorporated. As already discussed, the trapezoid is a very powerful geometric design that has built up static energy. This particular trapezoid is further 'frustrated' by being surrounded by triangles on both of its sides as well as its base, while the whole is a triangle, yet none on its top, where energy would flow more smoothly. This agitated trapped energy can be compared to sexual frustration; the trapezoid being representative of the male, while the missing or unaligned triangle that is to complete the union represents the female, being placed just out of reach. If union were to be achieved, a 'release' of static energy would then be radiated out of the now complete triangle. This is why the triangle is such a powerful force within esoteric magical work, it is a union of opposites into one flowing form, duality becoming one as is represented in the Baphomet.

Of course all of these geometric designs (three triangles and a trapezoid) are within one large triangle, sealing and concentrating the built up static energy of all within is borders.

Within the trapezoid a fire is to be built so the pure elemental essence of the flame may be made manifest, truly concentrating great elemental force within the Triangle in combination with the static energy of the combined geometric designs, creating a true portal and link to 'The Eternal Black Flame'. The Magician should be within the Triangle of Arte, in the large triangle below the trapezoid to recite the conjuration.

THE CONJURATION:

"I call to the Eternal Black Flame,
The Obsidian Fire that ever burns deep within the heart of Chaos,

I conjure the essence of the Abyss, the lifeblood of the Blackness,
Come forth and 'Be' the Flames within the Infernal Trapezoid before me.

Devouring Light of never ending Wisdom,
Burning Flame of All,
Come forth on this Night before the Stars…

Searing Darkness that guards the pure gnosis of Truth,
I conjure you forth to burn magnificently before me,
To forever be a representation of the Divine Spark of Illumination,
That resides within my flesh, as well as without.

Scorching essence of Chaos,
I call you forth to raise the black flames
within me to match your blinding brilliance,
I call you forth to engulf me in your Unholy Black Light,
I call you forth to cleanse me with your purity in Darkness.

Destroyer of Lies,
Guardian of Truth,
Spirit of Darkness...

Come forth and flow through me as Fire in my veins,
Blazing with a ferocity that has no equal.

Spirit of the Eternal Black Flame,
I call you forth !

Unholy Ghost of the Abyss,
I call you forth !

Divine Darkness of Light,
I call you forth !

This conjuration should be recited three times with true reverence. Once recited the Magician should meditate, clearing his mind of all internal dialogue, feeling The Eternal Black Flame burning brightly within. The fire should be allowed to burn out on its own, thus ending the rite. As the fire burns down, the Eternal Black Flame within the Magician grows stronger, until all the energy has been transferred from the physical fire to the spiritual within.

THE SEVENTY-TWO INFERNAL DJINN

1. **MAHMAS** – Appears as a tall and confident man having a goats head. He has long black hair that hangs down past his chest. He resides in the deep shadows of holy places, showing his powers are not restrained by the powers of Order. He is known to cause overall general distress and chocking to his victims resulting in painful death. His sigil is:

2. **MUNIS** – Appears as a tall man having only one eye, with the cloven feet of a mule. A black serpent is entwined around him, a sign of the powers of Chaos. He resides in lonesome graves and desecrated burial grounds. When he attacks his victims he changes his appearance to that of a black viper. He causes painful death like that of one dying of a venomous snake bite. His sigil is:

3. **NAQIQ** – Appears as a beautiful woman with long black hair, having the body of a large and powerful lion. She resides in waters that lie along the shore lines of any coast. When she attacks her victims while awake, she causes paralysis. However when the victim is sleeping, she causes 'sinking death'. Her sigil is:

4. **MAJID** – Appears as a tall man with a canine's head. His left hand is that of a mans holding a large golden staff, and his right is that of a canine's. He resides in desolate and wild places and in ancient wells. When he attacks his victim, he causes inflammation of the stomach with pain so terrible, that it renders his victim senseless. His sigil is:

5. **JADHBAH** – Appears as a tall man with a single eye, having the powerful hind legs of a golden lion. He stares intently at the Magician when evoked. He resides in dark water filled canals. When he attacks his victim he causes paralysis, then feasts on the flesh and infects the blood while the victim lies helpless until death ensues. His sigil is:

6. **QEL** – Appears as a tall man holding a large black horn used for calling. He inhabits roads, both physical and dimensional, though is not the road itself. He causes extreme weight to befall his victim, giving the sensation of being crushed under a large boulder, leaving the victim paralyzed. His sigil is:

7. **ALGHUL** – Appears as a large black crow having human hands, and the legs and head of a mule. It has long matted dirty hair that hangs down to the ground. It resides in lonesome dark ruins and desolate rocky areas. When it attacks its victims it causes men to be lead astray, opening other paths that lead to ruin. Of course this can be taken literally or symbolically. His sigil is:

8. **SAJIZ** – Appears as a large black raven having human hands and the ears of a donkey. It resides in the extreme elevation of all mountains. When it attacks its victims it causes violent sickness and horrible disfiguring, spreading disease to engulf the victim's body. Its sigil is:

9. **ALRAW'AH / ALRU'H** – Appears as a large beautiful peacock wearing a grand golden crown, holding a herdsman's staff,
with a large colorful spread out tail. It resides in the dark depths of
caves, grottos and underground areas. When it attacks its victim
it causes extreme fright for three seemingly endless days without
rest, causing one to fear any light, leaving them in horrible darkness both of the mind and body. If not cured in three days time,
the victim's sight will become permanently damaged or lost. Its
sigil is:

10. **MDYAN** – Appears as a tall man having one eye, with the body of a blackened serpent. He holds a drawn silver bow poised to strike. He resides in the waste and rubble of men. When he attacks his victim he causes painful paralyzation and complete loss of bodily control, then enters them as a serpent, possessing them for up to three years. His sigil is:

11. **LATUSH** – Appears as a dark hooded monk with long black hair, having a crow upon his head. He holds an elaborate golden staff in his left hand. He inhabits islands that reside cradled within the seas. When he attacks his victims he causes painful strangulation until death. His sigil is:

12. **ALDULAT WA HIRAM ALSEBYAN** – Appears as a woman from the waist down, the remaining upper half is that of hideous a seven headed goat with black human hair that hangs down to the ground. She carries a scared boy in her arms. She inhabits all mountainous regions. When she attacks her female victims, she attaches to the skin of a pregnant woman until she gives birth, then she painfully pinches the child until it bleeds, whereupon she feeds on it. Upon feeding she infects the child with a putrid sickness that leaves it horribly disfigured until painful death ensures. This particular Djinn is striking in appearance. Her sigil is:

13. **ALUQ** – Appears as two beings embracing one another, though joined in one form; one a hideous diseased man, and the other a beautiful woman with large black bat wings upon her back. The right leg is that of a mule, while the left a powerful lions. They reside in thick bushes and brush as well as in desolate ruins. When they attack their victims, they cause extreme fright until insanity ensues. Their sigil is:

14. **DANHASH** – Appears as a massive silver lion with sharp black horns, clenched between his fangs is the head of a man. He resides in all darkness upon the Earth. When he attacks his victims he causes darkness to befall them, their blindness leads them to see horrible dark phantomous beings and shades. He also resides within the womb, causing the loss of pregnancy due to the victims excessive lust for intercourse. His sigil is:

15. **NAZJUSH BENT DANHASH** – Appears as a beautiful woman having a single foot, and four human hands. She carries two vicious knives. She inhabits abandoned run down bathrooms. She has two ways of attacking her victims depending on their sex; if the victim is a man she causes delirium and heart complications. If a woman is her victim, she causes extreme sickness by covering her body. Her sigil is:

16. **ALDABAH / ALWAHENAH** – Appears as an enormous rugged man with the head of a normal sized man. His habitation is the deepest of seas. He attacks children, by causing sickness to them by way of blowing black disease into their nostrils. His sigil is:

17. **ALMUSRIF** – Appears as a fair woman with the head of a vicious canine, having long black human hair that hangs down to her waist. She resides in all holy temples, showing Order has no rule over her essence. When she attacks her victims she causes an extreme sense of pride, self importance, short temper and a want for solitude. Her sigil is:

18. ***ZOOBAGHAH** – Son of Iblis - One of the Dark Trinity that is
Iblis, Zoobaghah and Shara; Iblis, his son and daughter. Appears
as a tall bronze man with silver wings upon his feet, he rides upon
the back of a great beast resembling a dragon having two ferocious
fanged heads. He inhabits deep black canyons and valleys. He is
also known to reside at 'crossroads' and have the company of four
other unnamed Ifrit. When he attacks his victims, he strikes them
with violent blows causing terror and death by way of snapping
the victim's neck. His sigil is:

19. **ALHAJA** – Appears as a tall man having long black hair from the waist up, the remaining lower half is that of a powerful golden lion. He carries two gold staffs, one in each hand that have large red rubies on the end. He inhabits all areas of solitude and desolation. He attacks by corrupting the birth of children. His sigil is:

20. **AL'UIAH** – Appears as a blackened serpent having the head, hands and feet of a vicious canine. It resides in abandoned run down bathrooms and diseased wells. When it attacks women it causes them to appear pregnant by entering their womb. It also causes them to have heart fluctuations, and positions itself between their shoulder blades, then 'melts' into their body, giving the unimaginable sensation of crawling ants throughout. Its sigil is:

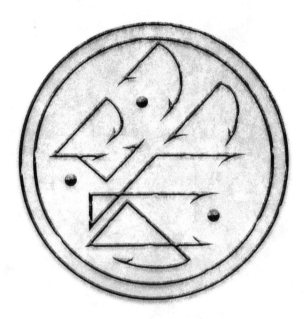

21. **BQAR DHAT ALASQAM** – Appears as a fair woman having the head as a fierce lion with long black hair, and elongated nasal trunk, like that of an elephant. She appears to have deformities. She resides in abandoned run down bathrooms. When she attacks pregnant women she causes them to loose their child by extending her trunk inside their womb. She then blows into the woman's pelvis, giving her the appearance of a man. Her sigil is:

22. **ALZUBDAH** – Appears as a tall man and woman with their heads and hands melting together. They are seen riding upon the back of a large camel. They reside in graveyards and follow funerals and the essence of death. They attack by blocking women from becoming pregnant. Their sigil is:

23. **ALQOOAH** – Appears as a large black raven having two heads; one the head of a peacock, and the other like that of a man. He stands large with extended black wings and is held fast by three large talons upon the ground. He resides within human mucus and attacks by causing the blood to become infected leading to mutation and deformation. His sigil is:

24. **ALSISAN** – Appears as a beautiful woman from the waist up with the lower half like that of a powerful lion. She carries a large black serpent in one of her hands. She resides in 'hidden areas' and abandoned bathrooms. When she attacks she causes depression and madness by resting on the edge of a drinking cup that the women use, entering their body. Her sigil is:

25. *QELNEMATAH – A great king of Djinn, faster and more dangerous than any other. He has full reign over all, being; lunar, gloomy, windy, terrestrial, celestial and cloudy. He appears in thirteen forms, being among them a great serpent, bull, canine, woman, horse, camel and a mule. He possesses seven heads, and mighty extended black wings. He inhabits the deepest regions of oceans. When he attacks his victims he causes seizures, strangulation and unconsciousness until control of the body is lost, causing suicide by way of throwing oneself from a cliff, or by some other form of self inflicted end. His sigil is:

26. **F'JYAN** – Appears in the form of a beautiful woman who has a golden collar round her neck and anklets upon her feet. She inhabits ancient tombs and places containing water. When she attacks she causes men to be enraged and women to go mad by hearing shrill, unstoppable, disembodied voices. Her sigil is:

27. **S'IH** – Appears as a beautiful woman having two long horns upon her head, with a tail like that of a monkey. A black serpent is entwined around her; a symbol of Chaos. She inhabits the deep forests upon the Earth, and places devoid of any presence or movement. She is a very powerful Djinn to use against Order, as she moves in the veins of the children of Adam, whispering of greed, alcohol, self importance, lust and all things that would bring death by their own hand. Her sigil is:

28. **ALRUAH** – Appears as a tall man with a black horses head, having large black wings upon his feet. In his left hand he carries a large iron bar. He is the trade master among the Djinn. He inhabits the coastline of all seas. When he attacks his victims he causes them to rip off all clothing until nothing remains. When the new moon is in phase, he causes extreme melancholy and obsession with the dead until the victim is 'drawn down' and joins them. His sigil is:

29. **ALQARSA** – Appears as a great wet fish, with a face like that of a human. Little is known of this Djinn. His sigil is:

30. **RUIMNAH** – Appears as a beautiful woman with two curled horns upon the head and large black wings. On her back is also the face of a woman. She resides in ancient ruins of all kinds. She does not attack her victims the way other Djinn do; instead, she seduces and possesses the minds of young men to do her bidding. Her sigil is:

31. **ALEKHNAMEN** – Appears as a tall man with the head, hands and feet of a great lion. He inhabits medicine of all types. When he attacks his victims he causes men to be stripped of all reason, understanding and comprehension. If a man starts to understand, ALEKHNAMEN distances his mind from it. He also causes painful strangulation. His sigil is:

32. **HABSHAHESH** – Appears as a tall man having a mule's head and two large white feathered wings upon his back. He inhabits homes. When he attacks his victims, he flows in them like the flow of their blood, whispering until madness ensues, leaving his victim helpless. His sigil is:

33. **LAHIF** – Appears as a tall man with a head like that of a ferocious monkey, having the feet of a canine. He inhabits the deep of the seas. When he attacks his victims, he possesses their mind and causes them heart fluctuations. He also causes fever, shivers and painful sickness. He overtakes his victims with whispers in the mind that seem like a warm wind. His sigil is:

34. **SMAHEL** – Appears as a tall man with a large black serpent entwined loosely around him; a symbol of Chaos. He holds in his left hand a mule's tail. He inhabits bridges and covered waterways. When he attacks his victims, he causes extreme strangulation and loss of the mind, where they run like a mad man until they cannot comprehend their own actions, nor where they are. His sigil is:

35. **BEQASMIN** – Appears as a tall man with the head of a vicious canine having two large black horns, two large black wings, and three eyes centered in his chest. He resides in the wombs of whores. When he attacks his victims, he causes painful death to those who have had their fill of alcohol and fallen asleep. His sigil is:

36. ALJUND' – Appears as a very large woman having the hands and feet of a canine. She inhabits roads often traveled. She causes extreme strangulation, throwing her victim to the ground in agonizing pain causing fierce convulsions and violent screaming. Her sigil is:

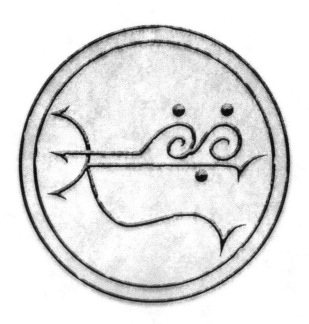

37. **TALYABA** – Appears as a tall black woman with one eye, having the fierce eyes of the crow, the nostrils of the canine, and the feet like that of the mule. She resides in all kinds of ancient ruins. When she attacks her victims, she causes extreme terror in both waking and in dream by attacking with the face of a hideous pig, lion, serpent and cat. Her sigil is:

38. **SEFIR** – Appears as an unattractive man with deformities to his face, he has a large spread peacock tail. He inhabits the peaks of large mountains. When he attacks his victims he causes them to become mentally unbalanced, inflicting both melancholy and laughter simultaneously. His sigil is:

39. **HAMUDI** – Appears as a woman having large black wings and one leg. She carries two black serpents in her hands; a symbol of Chaos. She inhabits wombs. When she attacks her victims she causes women to faint, have heart problems and cause harm to themselves. She also attacks infants by squeezing their hearts, sometimes until death. Her sigil is:

40. **ALNEFIS** – Appears in the form of a tall man, having the hoofs of a mule as hands. Upon him is entwined a black serpent; a symbol of Chaos. He inhabits all rivers and streams. When he attacks his victims he causes unrelenting sleeplessness, both day and night so no rest is given, driving his victims insane. His sigil is:

41. **HURTA** – Appears as a tall bearded man wearing a scarlet turban. He carries a large black serpent in his left hand; a symbol of Chaos. He resides in the hot coals of fire. When he attacks his victims he causes them to experience self importance, whispering, worry and terrible nightmares. His sigil is:

42. **ALRAHIAH** – Appears as a tall, very fair noble man with long black hair. He resides within the lungs. When he attacks his victims he causes extreme pain all over their body. His sigil is:

43. **ALDARBAN** – Appears as a tall man whose hands lock around his neck. He inhabits black wells and in deep caves. When he attacks women he causes false pregnancy pretending to be a fetus, causing confusion, delirium and madness. His sigil is:

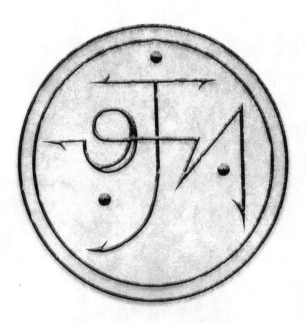

44. **ALKHATAF** – Appears as a tall man with large black wings, having the head of a raven. His form is stunning, being very beautiful and dusted in gold. He dwells outside the entryways of houses. When he attacks his victims he causes vomiting, fainting and rapid breathing, whispering and emotional distress. His sigil is:

45. **ALWISWAS** – Appears as a woman with two long black horns, long curved black wings, she stands upon seven feet. Tied around her waist hangs a noose that dangles behind her. She dwells in all forms of true darkness. When she attacks her victims she causes insanity, drunkenness and love of death. Her sigil is:

46. **YED UM MELDEM** – Appears as a very large fleshy woman, having yellowish skin and red hair. She inhabits the vast fields of fruit orchards. When she attacks her victims, she flows in them as blood rushing through their veins, relaxing them to paralyzation. Once done, she enters their flesh, leaving one crippled and forever tainted with her diseased essence. Her sigil is:

47. **ALZU'AH** – Appears as a weak limping man, holding his right leg in pain. He inhabits the seas. When he attacks his victims he causes extreme pain in the legs, knees and feet, leaving one forever disabled. His sigil is:

48. **ALNABAH** – Appears as a man having his right foot like that of a hoof, and the left like a lions. He resides at crossroads. When he attacks his victims he causes great depression and grief. His sigil is:

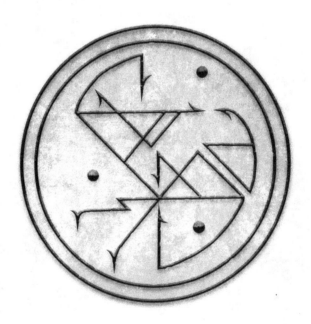

49. ALMUL – Appears as a beautiful woman with feet like that of a canine. There is a large black serpent on her back; a symbol of Chaos. She dwells in all ruins and run down areas. When she attacks her victims she causes insanity and depression, sometimes appearing as a canine or a blackened serpent, inflicting horrible various maladies. Her sigil is:

50. **ALWISWAS ALAKBAR** – Appears as a large man with the strong body of a tailless horse, having large black wings extended. He inhabits all mountainsides. When he attacks his victims he causes them to worry until it grows to the point of inflicting sleeplessness and the inability to describe the consuming concern, resulting in madness that overtakes the mind.

51. **ALKHANAS ALASGHAR** – Appears as a tall man with the head of a black ram. He dwells within the terror that stalks the night. When he attacks his victims he causes paralyzation and inflicts ulcers within the intestines, causing great pain and misery. His sigil is:

52. **ALHAMQA** – Appears as a woman with the head of a black canine, with deep set red eyes. She inhabits areas around seas. She causes the heart to slow to the point of near death, leaving one appearing dead to all who observe them. They are then buried and remain aware, unable to protest their burial. Once buried, ALHAMQA whispers and laughs in their coffin until the victim eventually dies. Her sigil is:

53. **HASEN** – Appears as a tall man with large black wings, he has the hands of a canine. He inhabits the courts of law. When he attacks his victims he causes strangulation and extreme pain to ones back and knees. His sigil is:

54. **ALMASUR** – Appears as a large, tall abomination of conjunctions; with a vicious monkeys head, a torso like an ant, and a mans legs. He resides in the blackest filth and waste. When he attacks his victims he causes sickness to the stomach by residing within it like feces. When he attacks his victims he causes sleeplessness and an inability to enjoy any pleasure in life. He inflames the body with a wild uncontrollable itch that cannot be relieved, and causes an attraction to wine. The Magician should be aware and warned, that although these entities all have their own foreboding dark presence, this particular Djinn is especially 'striking' and can cause great terror by simply manifesting. His sigil is:

55. **BALEM** – Appears as a tall man with large black wings, having a monkey's head and taloned bird feet. He dwells in all water. When he attacks his victims, he attacks extremely quickly and unseen, causing tearing of the flesh, disorientation, altered vision and unconsciousness. He restlessly attacks both night and day with swiftness. His sigil is:

56. **SHAKHYA** – Appears as a tall man with large white wings, having a head like a horned bull with one foot. He inhabits all water. When he attacks his victims he descends upon the sleeping, putting them into unwaking nightmare, then throws their body around, twisting and contorting it into horrible unnatural forms. In the waking hours the victim is lethargic and depressed. This Djinn attacks his victims in a way that very much resembles the state of a possessed person, performing bodily feats that one seemingly could not do under normal circumstances. His sigil is:

57. **BARDUN** – Appears as a short man with one eye, having the nostrils and feet of a duck. Resides in the cupboards of spell-casters and doctors. When he attacks his victims he takes the form of a wild canine and inflicts horrible vomiting and violent shivers causing seizures. His sigil is:

58. **BEZID ALMAJUSI** – Appears as a rugged man with the head of a canine, having small wings upon his feet. He dwells in all rivers. When he attacks his victims, He strikes only once, hard and strong, causing diarrhea along with extreme pain of the stomach. His sigil is:

59. **M'RUZ** – Appears as a tall single eyed man, with the feet of a canine. From within his open jaws is positioned another head that is human. He dwells in hills and mountain tops. When he attacks his victims he causes strangulation, and ceases the consumption of all food and drink. He tortures his victims for the period of one month. His sigil is:

60. **ALMLIAH ALNAFEDHA** – Appears as a large blackened serpent. He dwells alongside the 'sheep'. When he attacks his victims he causes severe headache and trauma, also causing heart troubles. His sigil is:

61. **MARWEYA** – Appears as a tall thin man having talons like that of an eagle. He dwells in mountains. When he attacks his victims he causes them to become lost, forever wandering the deserts and mountainsides. He causes his victim to eventually loose his mind as he looses his way, so no companionship may be found. His sigil is:

62. **ALFALIJ** – Appears as a tall man with large black wings, having a head like a monkey with a fierce gaze. He dwells among the hills. When he attacks men he strikes them from one side only, then sexually excites and drains their body of all seamen until they are painfully dried out. His sigil is:

63. **ALWATHEQ** – Appears as a tall man with large black wings, having the head of a horned bull. His presence is stunning. He inhabits churches and holy places. When he attacks his victims he causes his them to loose recognition of anyone or comprehend any words being spoken. His sigil is:

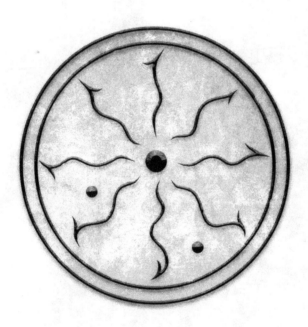

64. **ALS'ARI ALYAHUDI** – Appears as a short woman with the body of a shaggy black goat. She inhabits black wells and bodies of salted waters. When she attacks her victims, she bites on them until their flesh is infected and ignites their insides with what seems like fire, causing headaches and hallucinations. Her sigil is:

65. **LUQ** – Appears as a well kept man, having a beard and a gold crown upon his head. He dwells on the peaks of mountains. When he attacks his victims he causes strangulation and death in their sleep. His sigil is:

66. **ALMARIKH** – Appears as a tall noble man with large spread black wings. He appears wearing full golden armor and carrying a golden shield bearing his sigil. He inhabits ancient ruins and abandoned bathrooms. When he attacks his victims he causes strangulation, leaving them in a state between life and death, deceiving others that nothing has taken hold. This could be seen as a form of zombiefication, leaving one in an 'undead state'. His sigil is:

67. **MER ABU AL-SHISFAN SAHEB ALJEBEL MER** – Appears as a muscular man with his lower half being like a powerful lion. He covers his face with his hands so that his features may not be seen. He dwells in open markets and places where humans congregate. When he attacks his victims he causes infections of the eyes, depression, and distortion of their views on life. His sigil is:

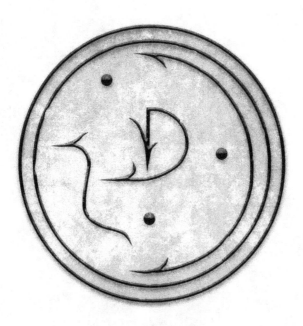

68. **ALHILYAH ALZAHERAH** – Appears as two massive winged mighty horses, one being larger, both having small heads. He inhabits the wilderness and vast dry lands. When he attacks his victims he causes swelling of the abdomen, heart problems, intense headaches and fever. His sigil is:

69. **QODSA** – Appears as a large black crow with a man's head, having also a gnawing head upon his back. He resides wherever there is the element of fire. When he attacks his victims he causes blindness to befall them. His sigil is:

70. **SHRAHI** – Appears as a tall well dressed man, wearing clothes of gold from the waist down. He has two small golden wings on his feet, and carries a large magical flat board, that changes symbols as he speaks. He dwells in the Syrian mountains. When he attacks women, he whispers to their hearts and causes them to disrobe. His sigil is:

71. **MAGHSHAGHAS** – He appears as a magnificent mighty golden lion with the face of a beautiful woman. He dwells among ruins and mountains. He attacks his victims by slaying male unborn children and causes separation between man and wife. His sigil is:

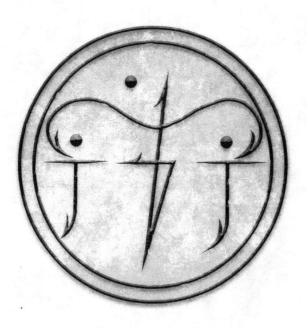

72. *SHARA* – Daughter of Iblis – One of the Dark Trinity that
is Iblis, Zoobaghah and Shara; Iblis his son and daughter. Appears as a beautiful woman with the head of a black raven, having
two black horns protruding from her head. She resides in the air.
When she attacks her victims she causes heart problems and also
projects ideas of grandeur into their minds, causing them to excite themselves into an ecstatic frenzy until their heart fails. Her
sigil is:

IBLIS

THE THREE CLASSES OF DJINN

The Djinn that are presented in this volume are not what I would consider truly 'evil'. They are evil in the sense that they serve no other purpose than to afflict pain and death, however are much needed as a source of pure Chaotic essence to overthrow the suppression of Order, and in this sense, they are 'good'. I am not anti-cosmic, nor against creation in the form of the Eagle's Emanations, I simply feel that the force of Order is overwhelming that of Chaos, and this suppression is what is 'evil'.

One of the forms Order takes is through Judeo/Christian religious dogma, controlling and suppressing all it can, until All is in perfect Order. The Djinn presented here are to be set free to destroy these restricting chains of the forces of Order, to combat them with raw brutal, untamed power. By releasing these beings, the Magician is releasing spiritual cut throat mercenaries onto the forces of Order, so that lost ground may be reclaimed. It is like burning a diseased forest to ashes, so that new pure growth may again rise from the Earth, strong and renewed. There is a disease of control and Order upon the earth that must be cleansed, the balance must be regained.

THE FIRST CLASS OF DJINN do not kill outright, though their victims may have rather well chosen death, over some of the horrendous and torturous acts these Djinn inflict upon their human quarry. Death is not the worst thing a human can experience; these Djinn know this and exploit this knowledge to the fullest. These particular Djinn make up the main body of the seventy-two, containing fifty-three in total. They are:

QEL, ALGHUL, SAJIZ, ALRAW'AH, MDYAN, ALUQ, NAZJUSH
BENT DANHASH, ALDABAH, ALMUSRIF, AL'UIAH, ALQOOAH,
ALSISAN, F'JYAN, S'IH, ALRUAH, ALEKHNAMEN, RUIMNAH,
HABSHAHESH, LAHIF, SMAHEL, ALJUND, TALYABA, SEFIR,
ALNEFIS, HURTA, ALRAHIAH, ALKHATAF, ALWISWAS, YED UM
MELDEM, ALZU'AH, ALUABAH, ALMUL, ALWISWAS ALAKBAR,
ALKHANSAS ALASGHAR, ALHAMQA, HASEN, ALMASUR,
BALEM, SHAKHYA, BARDUN, BEZID ALMAJUSI, M'RUZ,
ALMLIAH ALNAFEDHA, MARWEYA, ALFALIJ, ALWATHEQ,
ALS'ARI ALYAHUDI, MER ABU AL-SHISFAN SAHEB ALJEBEL
MER, QODSA, SHRAHI, SHARA, ALQARSA

THE SECOND CLASS OF DJINN are deadly. They kill in cold blood, no mercy is known or acknowledged in them, they are true killers waiting to be set free. Their total number is eleven. They are:

MAHMAS, MUNIS, NAQIQ, MAJID, JADHBAH, LATUSH,
ZOOBAGHAH, QELNEMATAH, BEQASMIN, LUQ, ALMARIKH

THE THIRD CLASS OF DJINN are unique in that they concentrate on pregnant women, causing death or deformation among other atrocities. They number eight in total. They are:

ALDULAT WA HIRAM ALSEBYAN, DANHASH, AL-
HAJA, BQAR DHAT ALASQAM, ALZUBDAH, HA-
MUDI, ALDARBAN, MAGHSHAGHAS

It can be seen that the Magician would apply the correct Djinn, or class of Djinn to the circumstance at hand, each Djinn is unique and has its own personal Chaotic touch. The vast amount of horrors that these Djinn can accomplish is unnumbered, there are many. It is easy for the Magician to be able to select the specific and correct Djinn for the act of bane that is to be carried out, with a particular victim in mind. Essentially there are so many applications and diversity, that this system is easily customizable to exactly what the Black Magician wishes to accomplish.

RITES OF EVOCATION

o begin, the Magician must first have decided which Djinn is needed, that he wishes to summon. In making this choice one must consider the landscape that is available to them, and where the specific Djinn may be found. No, this isn't convenient, and you cannot perform all the rites within your bedroom, unless applicable. If specific Djinn are only found along coastlines, you must go to a coastline to summon them. Though many Djinn perform very similar 'deeds' and have various locations in which they may be found, so finding one that suits your needs along with an accessible environment should be a task that can be fulfilled without too much trouble.

The Magician must locate an appropriate location to perform the rite and lay out the Triangle and Circle of Arte that he feels will best suit his needs. Any combination of Triangles and Circles may be used, giving the Magician a wide range of customization which is not normally available. The Triangles and Circles tend to be rather large, though no specific size is given, so use your best judgment. Take your time to draw the lines of the Triangles and Circles well, remember, angles are key in this system for success, they must be drawn correctly (straight) to be effective. Also, when tracing the lines, focus on what the Triangle is going to be used for and your goal of evocation.

Once the Triangle is drawn, find a central point or apex where many lines meet, and trace an outline of whichever hand you use to project personal energy, on that central point. It is here where you will push your personal energy into the Triangle, activating it and filling it with your personal energy when in ritual.

When you have completed the Triangle, you must now focus your energy on constructing the Circle. As with the Triangle, focus your energy on the Circle's function and visualize it as an amplifier and storehouse of energy. However, first you may wish to visualize it as an impenetrable fortress that none can breach. Again, take your time to lay the lines. This should be a meditative process, much like creating a Zen garden is, not rushed, but with focus. From my experience, I have found it best to lay out the Triangle and Circle one day, and return the next to perform the rite. A great deal of energy goes into the construction of these vehicles which leaves the Magician drained by their completion. Of course this is the opposite effect of what the rite is designed to do, so to return refreshed and energized is best. If this isn't possible do to time constraints, I advise laying out the Triangle and Circle, meditating awhile, and then performing the rite.

After the Triangle and Circle have been laid down, begin by placing your magical tools, sigils, etc. within. The Triangle should contain the brass lamp with the named incense at the ready which rests upon the Djinn's sigil which can be painted on a mirror, parchment or other surface. The Circle is to contain a simple altar which can be made of wood or stone that all other tools will rest on. Of course this can also be sigilized with Lunate Script. On the right side of the altar rests the scepter, on the left, the brass incense burning dish. The sword can rest on your side at the ready, and will be drawn before the evocation begins. After all, surround the area with enough candles to see, but not so many as to make it bright. At this point the rite has been fully prepared, and the Black Magician may begin when ready, though it is advised that the ritual begin after midnight and end before five in the morning. It is in these small hours of the night that the veil is thinnest and contact can be more easily made. The interference of the mundane is at its lowest level.

Light the incense within the Triangle, return to the Circle and sit comfortably behind the altar. Light the incense there and add two strips of the Words of Power which should have evocation commands and sigils written upon them. This is an example of strips used for calling forth ZOOBAGHAH:

"Come forth ZOOBAGHAH", "In the name of IB-
LIS, I (N.N.) call you forth to be before me ZOOBAGHAH",
"ZOOBAGHAH ZOOBAGHAH ZOOBAGHAH"

At this point the magician must cumulate his personal energy within the Circle, it is important to draw it all out and bring it forth to circulate around and through the lines of the Circle, surrounding the Magician in energy and strength. Visualize this energy as silver waves or strings swirling around the inside of the Circle. As stated the lines of the Circle are designed to strengthen the energy that is being released by the Magician, resulting in a mass of bursting personal energy, spinning around the Magician waiting to be directed. Meditate on feeling this energy surround and spin around you, feel the earth move under you, know you wield true power. When you 'know' you have reached an energetic climax, visualize all the silver spinning energy enter your body through your back between your shoulder blades, filling you with strength and the gnosis of being.

Walk out of the circle to the Triangle, personal blood sacrifice is now made and presented in the sacrificial offering bowl. It is at this point when personal energy is at its highest peak within you, that your blood is charged and most potent. When you feel you can no longer contain the surging energy, push all of that spinning silver internal energy out through your hand into the Triangle through the outlined handprint already laid. Visualize a huge surge of energy being pushed from you into the Triangle, and rapidly spreading out through all the lines until they are pulsating with silver power. The Triangle is now activated and flowing with energy waiting to be snapped and the barriers broken. Once done, return to the Circle.

Add more incense and two more strips of Words of Power to the coals and return to a standing position. Holding your scepter in your left hand and your sword in your right, positioned across your chest so that the blade touches your left shoulder, call the Djinn forth that you require. As described, vibration is a key element in the success of this system, however, so in Intent. Be loud when you recite the evocation, but most importantly you must infuse your words and vibrations with true meaning and emotion. Being that these particular entities are only of pure wrath, I can only imagine one infusing their words with the emotion of hatred and anger, wishing to utterly destroy the target subject in mind. The evocation is to be recited three times with reverence,

"(Djinn's Name Repeated In Three Sets Of Seven, In Low Guttural Voice),

I call out to the Blackest Spirits that roam the
darkest recesses of the hidden Earth !
Spirits that seethe and slither in shadowed timeless chambers unseen,

I call out to the ancient one of the bloody house of Taw ~ All !
Who despises the burning Holy Light of Order,

I summon forth (Djinn's Name), from the blackest
pits of nightmare to be present before me,
I call forth (Djinn's Name) in the name of the Unholy father IBLIS, to be
made manifest in terrible visible form within the Triangle of Spaces,

(Djinn's Name Three Times), Hear my voice, Hear My Voice !
Come to me warrior of old, whose heart is filled with boundless anger,

Come forth (Djinn's Name) !
Fill this temple with your sinister presence !

I call to you with the purest rage ablaze from within,
I call to you with the purest hatred for those who love the Light,

(Djinn's Name), I call to you in this twilight hour,
This hour of forsaken silence,

(Djinn's Name), I summon you forth from the
Abyss of terror that is your abode,
I call you forth from the clan of Taw ~ All to strike
pain and death into my enemy (N.N.),

(Djinn's Name), Come forth and release your hatred
onto the one who has come against me !
Bring them dark shadows of unearthly fright,

(Djinn's Name), I summon you forth from the desolate wastes of Jahannam,
I call you from the smokeless fire, from which you are composed,

(Djinn's Name Three Times), Spirit of darkness manifest !
Become in the Triangle of Spaces !

Manifest !

This evocation is strong and has proven itself effective; it does what it is designed to do. Once the Djinn has made itself known, remember to stand strong, though this can be easier said then done. Even if one is not clairvoyant enough to visibly see the Spirit with their eyes, its presence is unmistakable. The entire area will become 'darker', and a strange weight will fill the air. It will feel like the world has stopped, like time and space, reality and non-reality are no longer in motion. For this brief, frozen, stolen moment in existence…there is only the Djinn and yourself. Greet the Djinn in an honorable way,

"Greetings (Djinn's Name) I (N.N.) welcome you here as a warrior and equal in this Temple, and am honored by your presence."

It is at this point that the Djinn may ask why it has been called it forth, state your reason and direct it to your desired target. Add two more strips of Words of Power and Incense. It must be remembered that these entities are not friendly, and cannot be made allies that will genuinely look out for you. They only work with you to satisfy their own ravaging hunger.

Once you have stated your reason for calling, thank the Djinn for its appearance and the deeds it is about to unleash on your target victim, being sincere, but short if you don't wish to bond. Prolonged exposure to these entities causes the Magician to breathe them 'in'. These effects can be desired, but expect a 'dark shift' to occur within the psyche. This communion can be utilized to gain in personal strength, allowing for greater Black Magic to be performed, as these entities are of the raw force of Chaos itself. After you have thanked the Djinn, simply state,

"My Intent has been directed, and you are now unleashed upon the world and my target victim, I thank you for your action, (N.N.), we are now done here."

The rite has been performed; there is no banishing to be put into place. When completed, stay in the Circle for at least thirty minutes, burn the last two strips of Power Words and incense. In this time, contemplate and visualize the damage that is now occurring to your victim, see the Djinn surrounding them, performing its tasks you have set upon it. Also take this time to relax yourself; these communions can be stressful to the nervous system.

The same Djinn may be called as many times as the Magician requires, but as stated, repeat contact and communion has its effects. It is best as with all Spirits to be specific with your Intent when stating it. As an example if you say you wish the Djinn to attack your enemy, state when or within how many days time. Else, it could be a year from when you were expecting the damage to occur. Though, as said, they are their own masters, and do as they wish. The Black Magician does not command them, but directs them.

CONJURATION OF IBLIS

blis...Shaitan, The First Opposer, the one to first speak out against Order. The first one to say 'No, I reject the reality I am being presented and forced into'. He is a figure head, a mask, an anthropomorphic face for the raw energy of Chaos. Chaos has many faces, as does Order. One must realize that all the faces of Chaos share the same 'body', all the different rivers have the same source. Shaitan is an ancient name for Chaos, He has been worked with for centuries, honored by the truthful, feared by the ignorant and weak. To be born of Chaos means to be born a lone wanderer in this world full of those who would gladly be food for a corrupted force. It means to walk alone amongst the blind, to be a lone wolf amongst the sheep...that wishes to devour the 'Sheppard' who keeps all in line.

Iblis is the Father...He is Lucifer, Satan, Samael, Shaitan, The Dark Lord. He is Commander of the Djinn. He can be accessed by all who have a deeper understanding of the multiple faces of Chaos. He is an ancient source who has many applications to the Black Magician. I have included here a simple, yet powerful evocation dedicated to Him,

Iblis...

Demon Angel of Darkness, Opposer of the False Light,
I call you forth from the starless Abyss...

Iblis...

Father of lone Nightshades, Destroyer of the Great Illusion,

I call you forth from your hollowed sanctuary...

I call you forth from the Blackness of My Heart,
Father, Bless me with your presence,

Come forth and embrace this venerated land,
Come forth and behold the glory I shower upon you,

Iblis..!

I call you to stand before me in all your Infernal Might,
I summon you forth from hidden spaces of the Earth !

Iblis Hear My Voice !

Iblis See Thy Veneration !

Iblis Taste My Blood !

Iblis Smell Thy Incense !

Iblis Feel My Anger !

Iblis Come Forth !

I who am of the True Chaos Spirit call you forth from dark-
ened lands to bestow upon me your blessing,
I who walk in Death's Shadow summon you to commune with me, to guide me, to embrace me.

I your unholy son, call you, my unholy Father...

Destroy mine enemies; bring down upon
them your hatred of the mundane,
Wipe them from the face of the Earth,
Cover them with burning blisters,

Curse them to eternal pain,
Scar thy name upon their skin,
For they deserve your wrath,
Iblis…

Master of all Djinn,

Lord of all Chaos,

I call you forth,

Father of the Sinister !

I call you forth !

~ I ~ B ~ L ~ I ~ S ~

Come Forth…

Final Word

s a young child I recall having thought; 'what if everyone around me were not real, but simply there to fool me, so 'they' could watch my reactions to various situations'. I didn't fully trust that the people around me were 'genuine'. Who would do this, I did not know, though then again, how could one if they truly are immersed in a non-reality, reality ? I remember having this thought repeatedly, or I should say that the thought would periodically reoccur from time to time throughout my childhood years on into my adult life. I hold this thought to still be somewhat true, though it has grown far more complex over the years.

Reflecting on this, I ask myself, where did I get such an idea with no outside influence ? How was I aware of the concept, that perhaps I was in a simulated reality at such a young age ? I see this now with open eyes, and know that one is either born of Order or of Chaos; it is not a choice. This was taught to me by a good friend and mentor of sorts. I am born of Chaos, and I understand now, that I have brought with me into this incarnation, collective knowledge of my previous existences. I find it quite interesting, and more than compelling that I did/do have these thoughts, that somehow I came 'here' with them already instilled/programmed within me. I know now, this is the essence of Chaos that exists within the 'awake'. It is an ingrained truth that exists within the construct of ones very being. Some could call this accessing ones 'Holy Guardian Angel' or higher self, though I do not see it as such, but as tapping into oneself and receiving the pure truth that resides inside, untainted by the illusion that surrounds. It is born Gnosis...

My 'reality' is my own, and still, I do not believe it to be 'real', as I can no longer define what is real. What is 'real' is left up to the individual. Who is to say what is real ? How can one define what is real ? With all the scientific and magical advancements, who can definitively say what is possible ? It is a ridiculous concept that is limiting, if one only spends the time to consider it. One of my most cherished quotes from H.P. Lovecraft perfectly captures the essence of that, which I am speaking,

> *"...All life is only a set of pictures in the brain, among which there is no difference betwixt those born of real things and those born of inward dreaming, **and no cause to value one above the other.**"*
> H.P. LOVECRAFT, *'THE SILVER KEY'*

I believe in the Consensual Reality Matrix. The Consensual Reality Matrix is Order. It is the sustained illusion that 'all' around us is 'real' and tangible. It is sustained mostly by the mundane; those who will never 'see' or awaken from their dream, only to be recycled again and again. And perhaps my childhood thoughts are true, that when I watch my neighbors go into their houses, they cease to exist until it is time again for them to reappear and perform their functions; to sustain 'the illusion'. I believe that the energy that creates this 'reality/illusion' can be tapped into and manipulated/reprogrammed. The way this happens is through the science of magic. Once we get past the general connotations one normally associates with Magic, we can see it for what it is; an energetic working that is pushed out into the energy field that is the Consensual Reality Matrix to change/rewrite it to a Magician's specific needs. Magicians are reality manipulators, and no, this is not looked upon with welcoming eyes from the 'system' that is the Consensual Reality Matrix/Illusion. It has been said by Magicians that when they started practicing Magic that they had horrible things occur to them, bad luck so to speak. Many will abandon their practice at this point and return to their Christian roots and find happiness in slavery. However for those who were strong and kept on, they gained in personal power through each working, and the 'bad luck' calmed down, though never is entirely removed. However, this 'bad luck' is the Consensual Reality Matrix's defense system. It will manipulate your reality to make it difficult for you to continue on your own 'independent' path; the path of enlightenment where you become awake and can 'see' the reality around you for what it is; a system that can be changed. In other words, if you step out of line of what you are intended/programmed to do, if you start to think for yourself, become self aware and go against the grain, if you begin to rewrite the code of 'reality' through energy working, expect the system's security to try and smack you back into place. It will do this with all it can, be it finances, death or in some cases luxury. Anything that will distract you from independence and independent thought, anything that will make you focus back on the mundane world of the illusion. If you are aware of this going in, you will easily see these unfortunate 'coincidences' as the defense system I am speaking of. However, this is a positive result because it will indicate to you that you are on the right path and that you are already strong enough to be seen as a threat to the structure of the Consensual Reality Matrix. I can only say that if this is occurring to you, press on, it doesn't get easier, but you will be free, and if enough of us awaken, we can change it all.

My 'reality' is different than yours. This is based upon my collective experiences, which I must say, have been quite different than most others. Each of us has our own 'reality'; no two realities are the same despite their likenesses. Therefore, before one can manipulate their 'reality' through Magic, one must first come to understand the 'reality' in which they dwell; know the rules, how things work. This can be difficult as when one first starts out upon this journey, there are many who would guide them astray by saying that 'reality' is like 'this', or like 'that'. One cannot be misguided by these words and descriptions, for they are the author's own view of 'his' reality, which cannot be completely yours. This being said, one can relate to another and hold the same beliefs, but understand that you will never view something completely in the same way, or connect and hold the same emotions and values to a subject, event or object as the other/s. This is because we are not all the same, and each have had different experiences and learned different values from one another at different times. Some are deep while others are shallow; all depends upon experience, in whatever form it takes to teach. In order to practice Magic, one must first understand their personal 'reality' and its set of rules so that they may be bent or broken and the Magician manipulate the Consensual Reality Matrix in their personal favor. Knowing your 'reality' cannot be taught, you must push *your own* boundaries to gain *your own* understanding of where *you* are; no one can teach you this.

In my reality, Order and Chaos are on the 'board/field/grid', infused within the very programming of the Consensual Reality Matrix, ever raging against one another. Throughout 'time' the struggle shifts balance, giving one more power than the other. Currently Order is the stronger force, locking down any form of originality, free form thought and expression. Thus, Chaos must have a surge of raw chaotic energy to give it the power it needs to fight back. This book is a weapon against Order.

It is my hope that my releasing of this manuscript be understood and seen as an act of war in the chance for a new peace in this reality that is my own, but recognize some others view as well. If I didn't feel these entities could help fight the ever controlling and restraining forces of Order, I would never have released this text. If I didn't think that the time was now, 2013C.E that this text was needed, this manuscript would never have been brought forth. The world is being repressed; creativity stomped out, freedom being taken away. It is my hope that this work be seen as a most terrible weapon, to be used against those controlling forces of Order so that diversity, free will and the exploration of what 'could be', may be allowed to exist. We must break down the walls that are being built up that suppress 'living' and the ability to have choice. This tome is an expression and embodiment of this eternal struggle, an expression of the fight for freedom, free thought and free will.

The entities in this text that are to be brought forth are of the purest, blackest, manifestations of Chaos that there are. They are of their own reality. As I have said, Chaos is pure potential, unbounded by any restraint, and while this is a positive aspect of this undefined force, there is also the side of it that is of pure destruction. That side has no understanding of mercy, no thought of restraint or remorse. This raw energy is extremely powerful and not to be trifled with. It is to be released with Intent and let go to complete its task. Do not stand in its way.

These entities have been long waiting, scratching at the veil, and now in your hands lies the sword that will slash it open and part the way. I bid you farewell, may you use this devastating force when truly needed, and may your intentions be noble in its application, for we of the LHP must stand united if we are to again bring balance to this 'reality' that is being controlled by Order. Stand strong...

~ S. Ben Qayin

Smokeless Fire

CPSIA information can be obtained
at www.ICGtesting.com
Printed in the USA
BVHW060937090221
599641BV00003B/858